A
Psalm
FOR
Every
Season

A Psalm FOR Every Season

30 DEVOTIONS TO
DISCOVER ENCOURAGEMENT, HOPE AND BEAUTY

Arnold R. Fleagle

Illustrated by Timothy R. Botts

Chosen

a division of Baker Publishing Group
Minneapolis, Minnesota

© 2022 by Arnold Fleagle

Published by Chosen Books
11400 Hampshire Avenue South
Minneapolis, Minnesota 55438
www.chosenbooks.com

Chosen Books is a division of
Baker Publishing Group, Grand Rapids, Michigan

Printed in the United States of America

Library of Congress Cataloging-in-Publication Data
Names: Fleagle, Arnold R., author. | Botts, Timothy R., illustrator.
Title: A Psalm for every season : 30 devotions to discover encouragement, hope and beauty / Arnold R. Fleagle ; illustrated by Timothy R. Botts.
Description: Minneapolis, Minnesota : Chosen Books, a division of Baker Publishing Group, 2022. | Includes bibliographical references.
Identifiers: LCCN 2022009892 | ISBN 9780800762681 (hardcover) | ISBN 9781493437665 (ebook)
Subjects: LCSH: Bible. Psalms—Prayers and devotions.
Classification: LCC BS1430.54 .F54 2022 | DDC 242/.5—dc23/eng/20220316
LC record available at https://lccn.loc.gov/2022009892

Cover design by Dan Pitts
Cover and interior art by Timothy R. Botts
Interior design by William Overbeeke

Author represented by Wordwise Media Services

Baker Publishing Group publications use paper produced from sustainable forestry practices and post-consumer waste whenever possible.

22 23 24 25 26 27 28   7 6 5 4 3 2 1

I dedicate *A Psalm for Every Season* to Dr. Lawrence "Larry" Bradshaw, my class advisor, my English and creative writing instructor, and a committed Christian who modeled Jesus with his lips and his life. Mr. Bradshaw's enthusiasm for my writing potential and his prompting me to express my ideas on paper extended even to his writing a letter to my parents, Ralph and Crene Fleagle, so they would be cheerleaders to motivate me to make my writings public. His influence, more than any other person, enhanced my compositions and emboldened me to publish.

Contents

FOREWORD

I have known Pastor Arnold R. Fleagle personally for many years. This accomplished preacher and writer is, most importantly, a shepherd who deeply cares for the people Jesus died to save. We know this firsthand by his tender care of my family through many hours, prayers and visits to the hospital as we held on tight to loved ones. I am honored to say I know him as a real and genuine friend, and I am honored to write the following words about his book *A Psalm for Every Season*.

The Psalms were the Jewish songbook, the first hymnal, if you will. As a gospel singer, I have been drawn to the Psalms my whole life. To sing your faith is a wonderful gift. God's people sing! We do not stop with laments and cries for help. No, ultimately all things lead to praise, thanksgiving and singing because of our wonderful Savior! Oh, what a Savior He is.

I have read *A Psalm for Every Season* many times as a guide. Pastor Fleagle has the unique ability to use words that open the eyes of my heart to see things with fresh insight. True spiritual wisdom will do that for any seeker. And as a person who has spent a lifetime singing and ministering through song, I am so grateful to have this book to keep my heart in tune.

No matter what season of life you find yourself in, *A Psalm for Every Season* will lead you to your Savior and help you find your voice to sing, sing, SING!

Ernie Haase, Grammy-nominated
and Dove Award–winning gospel singer

ACKNOWLEDGMENTS

I am grateful to the Lord for opening the door for this writing endeavor (Revelation 3:7). In addition, I am thankful for my agent,
David Fessenden, who believed in the theme and content of this
work; for Timothy Botts, who invested his outstanding talents in
calligraphy and for his willingness to work with me again; and for
my wife, Faye, who joined with me in supporting this publication
of a book on the Psalms. Also, thanks to Chosen Books, which,
through its editorial director, Kim Bangs, and her staff, made the
finished product something that possessed clarity and flow!

INTRODUCTION

The word *psalms* in Hebrew means "praises"; in Greek it means "songs." Combine the two ideas and you will find that "praise songs" aptly describes the basic themes of the poetry and prose that Israel set to music and used as a hymnbook. The many writers of the Psalms (with David being the most prominent and prolific) were often harassed and hounded, confused and critical, but they eventually seemed to return to the summit of praise. So it should be in our pilgrimage: Though we taste of sorrow, we should finish our course with the sweet morsels of joy on our lips!

The classic men of the Bible ran to the Psalms for their inspiration in their greatest triumphs and tragedies. Jonah quoted them in the fish's belly; Jesus in the Garden of Gethsemane. Peter incorporated the Psalms into his marvelous Pentecostal sermon, and Paul included their wisdom in his Roman masterpiece. Maybe we should find our way there, too. These are ancient texts, but they are profitable for contemporary living.

I have now been praying through the Psalms for over three years. The insights that the Lord has shown me are precious to me, and I believe they could be significant for you, as well. John Calvin wrote that the Psalms consist of "an anatomy of the soul,"[1] and I believe their truth addresses virtually every facet of the human experience.

I invite you to join me in this journey through *A Psalm for Every Season*.

PSALM 1

My Counselor

Blessed is the man
    who does not walk in the counsel of the wicked,
nor stand in the way of sinners,
    nor sit in the company of scoffers.
Rather, his delight is in the law of the LORD,
    and on that law he meditates day and night.

Psalm 1:1–2 NCB

THE OPENING PSALM of the Hebrew hymnbook is a theological divide: The first three verses are devoted to the saint, the next three to the sinner. It forms one of the Bible's most promising texts for believers, and one of the most punishing for unbelievers. There is no neutral ground, no demilitarized zone. You are either for God or against Him; an evergreen fruit tree or a piece of worthless chaff; bound for the Promised Land or headed for unthinkable punishment!

This psalm begins with the word *blessed*, which in the original language is in plural form, for emphasis—how many times

My Counselor

blessed is the one who avoids ungodly influences! But this positive beginning is followed swiftly on its heels by a warning about the power of negative associates and counselors. The axiom that in five years people will be products of the books they read and the friends with whom they associate is robustly endorsed by this psalm. Life is like a photograph—what and whom you leave out of the picture are just as important as what and whom you allow in it.

"Bad company corrupts good character" (1 Corinthians 15:33). One bad apple really does make the whole bunch bad. The first verse of Psalm 1 demonstrates that the progression of contact with the ungodly comprises a series of red flags—first people walk with the ungodly, then they stand and finally they sit down. What begins casually leads to conversation and ends in confinement. Our circle of friends, sooner or later, becomes our circle of counselors. Whether this is a good thing or a bad thing depends on the kind of friends we have. "As iron sharpens iron, so one man sharpens another" (Proverbs 27:17 LEB), but dull iron makes for dull iron.

One of the barometers of spiritual health is a person's love affair with God's Word. Psalm 1:2 paints a blessed individual as one who delights in God's Word in the daylight and through the night season. The blessed person assigns a place in his or her schedule for engagement with God's Word. Does your day start with a briefing from the Master's manual? Are you taking time to feed on His Word daily? The daily bread of the true believer is found in digesting the Word of God—and digestion takes time! The Bible must not be a quick-fix snack food, but a meal well chewed, enjoyed and savored.

This Bible is not a road map, but it is a compass, and every committed believer must be riveted to it and piloted by it, and not detoured by a culture that is heading down a dead-end street. His flawless law leads to a formidable faith. His Word is the premiere counselor, "a lamp to my feet, and a light for my path" (Psalm 119:105 WEB).

Compelling Thought

The answer to the question, "Who is my counselor?" also answers the question, "What is my destiny?"

Comforting Prayer

Dear Lord,

I realize that my companions have a large role in whether my life bears fruit or is barren. Please give me discernment as I choose my herds and huddles so that my journey will be favored by Your presence and Your sweet blessing. Enable me to influence others in such a way that I will be a help, not a hindrance, to their holiness and righteousness.

PSALMS 3 *and* 4

A Strategy for Sleep

I lie down and sleep;
> I wake again because the LORD sustains me.

> > > Psalm 3:5 CSB

I will both lie down and sleep in peace,
> for you alone, LORD, make me live in safety.

> > > Psalm 4:8 CSB

DAVID WAS THE MOST POWERFUL** personality of his era. As king of Israel, he embarrassed his people's enemies, extended the country's boundaries and escalated the nation's wealth. However, he reveals in Psalms 3 and 4 that he was threatened by many adversaries. It is noteworthy that in both of these psalms, his faith in the Lord and the protection the Lord provides him are demonstrated by *sleep*!

Sleep and rest are biblical trademarks of God's blessing. Psalm 127:2 declares, "[He] gives sleep to those he loves" (CEB). However, this blessing is not always easy to grasp. The many stresses of our modern age have interfered with the rest of many a believer. So many Christians toss and turn at night as they wrestle with realities that appear in a plurality of forms—sometimes human, sometimes natural, sometimes genetic, sometimes even demonic. The follower of Jesus Christ walks a narrow road lined with obstacles and opposition.

The superscription to Psalm 3 discloses that this writing occurred when David was fleeing from Absalom, his own son. Now, that's a prescription for wrinkled bedcovers! I cannot imagine one of my sons planning to force me out of my job so they could be named my successor, yet this was the case with David.

Absalom coveted his father's throne. He questioned his father's justice, charmed the people with politician's kisses and lured away Ahithophel, his father's counselor. Absalom deceitfully asked his father's permission to go to Hebron, all the time with the secret purpose of forming an army to overthrow David. Absalom, whose name means "father of peace," had become his father's most dangerous predator. Can you imagine how David felt when the messenger brought the shocking news that "the hearts of the men of Israel are with Absalom" (2 Samuel 15:13 AMP)?

How did David leverage this incredibly disturbing development to gain the strength to lead his people and be able to sleep at night? The two psalms contain his threefold strategy:

First, he passionately prayed (Psalm 3:4; 4:1; 4:3). David communicated loudly and often because he fully expected the Lord to respond to his petitions. Do we pray with expectancy or just with panic?

Second, he had a high view of his protector: "You, LORD, are a shield around me" (3:3 ISV). The original Hebrew means a shield that completely insulated the warrior-king. Is the Lord inclusive in

A STRATEGY FOR sleep

His protection of His people, or is He unable to secure our position? David understood what we must believe and live by—that nothing can reach us unless it passes through His holy hands.

Third, David committed himself to abandon fear (3:6) and tenaciously trust in the Lord (4:5). He put his confidence in the One who specializes in deliverance (4:8).

The Great Physician wrote this three-part prescription for David to prevent him from experiencing insomnia: (1) passionate prayer, (2) correct theology and (3) tenacious trust.

Jesus Christ made a beautiful offer to those who were worn out by the battle of life: "Come to me, all of you who are weary and burdened, and I will give you rest" (Matthew 11:28 csb). Come and experience sleep in the middle of troubled times. The anxiety, panic and torment over the difficulties of life yields little resolution or change. The Father and the Son are waiting for someone to call to Them, someone to understand who They are, someone to surrender the trouble to Them because they trust in Their power to conquer whatever or whoever surrounds them.

Augustine, the early Church father, once wrote, "Our heart is restless until it rests in Thee."[1] May we comprehend that unchanging reality. The many adversaries of David were overcome by his one ally—his loving God!

Compelling Thought

The answer to the question, "Who is my source of safety?" also answers the question, "How well do I rest?"

Comforting Prayer

Dear Father in heaven,

You are my Protector and Refuge. My life is challenged on many fronts, and at times, I look to myself and not to You. Forgive me for my independence and assist me in casting all my cares upon You and the Lord Jesus Christ. May I sleep well, knowing that You never sleep and that all things are small to You.

PSALM 8

Majesty

When I consider Your heavens,
    the work of Your fingers,
the moon and the stars,
    which You established,
what is man, that You are mindful of him?
    And the son of man, that You care for him?

Psalm 8:4–5 TLV

IN ALL LITERATURE there is no more concise statement on the comprehensive excellency of the Creator God than Psalm 8. The psalmist spans the galaxy from the constellations to the crib of a tiny child to demonstrate the majesty of the Lord God Almighty. It is a sweeping, breathtaking song of grand and glorious admiration and awe. This psalm is designated an "envelope song" because it begins and ends with the same exclamation: "O LORD, our Lord, how majestic is your name in all the earth!" (EHV).

Additionally, there is no more concise statement on the creatures we call human beings than in verses 4 through 8. In contrast to this incomparable God, we would seem to take an insignificant place in the universe. But this psalm contends that humankind is but a "hummingbird's eyelash" below an angel, and our position on the planet is akin to God's position in the universe, one of dominion, power and authority. Hold on to your suspenders! This psalm is an elevator to our feelings, not only about the God we adore, but about the race we belong to on earth.

This psalm is a gold mine of exulting God and elevating man. Like a master of ceremonies, it presents the King and His subjects, whom He has promoted from paupers to royal personalities. This psalm assists us in answering Augustine's prayer: "O God, may I know myself, may I know thee."[1]

The glory of God in this psalm crosses the universe with light speed. The tail end of verse one finds God's glory above the heavens. It is higher than we will ever reach on this earth. It is farther than we will ever travel, until we are taken in death or translated like Enoch or Elijah. His name is majestic in all the earth, but the earth is not sufficient to contain it; our planet is like a small glass trying to hold oceanic waters.

Then the glory of God streaks back to the nursery. The excellence of God is found in the incoherent "ga-ga goo-goos" of the diaper set. It is not the cuteness of the little tykes that is being showcased here, but the fact that God can employ little creatures to still great enemies of His Kingdom. The power and awesomeness of God is demonstrated in the weak things of this world. First Corinthians 1:27 notes this: "But God chose the foolish things of the world to shame the wise. He chose the weak things of the world to shame the strong" (ERV). The greatness of a personality is found in the weakness of those things in a person that God uses to get the job done.

When David faced Goliath, both the Philistine and Israeli armies must have labeled it the greatest mismatch of the ages. A gladiator from Gath named Goliath is challenged by a ruddy shepherd boy with a slingshot. Think back over David's words in 1 Samuel 17:45: "You come against me with sword and spear and javelin, but I come against you in the name of the LORD Almighty." Do you see the strategy of God? The higher the odds, the more dramatic the demonstration of His majesty!

In Old Testament times, when God wanted to pry Israel loose from four centuries of bondage in Egypt, He began with a baby hidden in the river. Moses, whose name means "out of water," was rescued by none other than Pharaoh's daughter. In the New Testament, when God wanted to reveal His Messiah and proclaim Him to the world, He picked a young lady in Nazareth of poor peasant stock. Mary conceived and delivered a baby in a small town called Bethlehem. What did you say was that baby's name? His name is Jesus!

As we face our giants and our empires, we should believe that even though we are outnumbered and the odds are stacked against us, God enjoys confounding the oddsmakers of this world. His glory is revealed in the cribs of this world!

Psalm 8 has been nicknamed "the astronomer's psalm." Most likely, David wrote it as he gazed upon the night sky and watched the stars wink at him. He is considering the heavens in verses 1 and 3. He is trying to imagine the incomprehensible God who has called him for service. He is surveying the incredible universe that God has designed and placed before all mankind to behold. The cribs of verse two are replaced with the constellations of verse three.

David was no different from the poets who have mused and dreamed about the night sky through the centuries. Many of us studied James Weldon Johnson's poem "The Creation," which reflects humankind's preoccupation with the unlimited universe that envelops us. The universe is a miraculous tribute to our God— and we know the Architect of the galaxies! We know the Designer of millions of worlds. We live in a galaxy powdered with planets and stars, each one a brilliant, shining tribute to our God!

At times we do feel like an atom in the immense cosmos, a single leaf, falling to the ground in history's forest, unnoticed and ignored, a grain of sand on the endless shores of eternity. But we must remember that God created us for a purpose, and He reached down to us in Jesus Christ.

Indeed, we are the visited race; this is the visited planet. And whatever inferiority complex has draped us, we must never forget God's love affair with us. He has made us, according to Psalm 8:5, in His image, with dominion and power over the plant and animal kingdoms. He has put "all things under [our] feet" (Psalm 8:6 isv). Someone once stated, "Every dish of fish or fowl that comes to our table is an instance of the dominion God has over the works of man's hands."[2]

Yes, we are human beings, in male and female version. Contrasted with God, we are infinitesimal, but He is the Potter, and potters take useless clay and manufacture masterpieces out of them. The Creator has spruced us up, and we creatures can change our world! So what if we think we are weak instruments? A toothpick driven by a tornado can dig its way into a tree. Don't underestimate what God can do with you or me!

Compelling Thought

The answer to the question "Can God use the ordinary to do the extraordinary?" also answers the question, "Can I be used in His divine plan even though I'm just an ordinary person?"

Comforting Prayer

Dear Lord Almighty,

The oceans seem so vast, and my ship seems so small. Yet, according to Your Word, I am just a little lower than the heavenly beings. Guide me through the waters of this world so that I may reach the shores of Your will for my life.

Day 4

PSALM 14

Believe

The fool says in his heart,
  "There is no God."
They are corrupt, their deeds are vile;
  there is no one who does good.

Psalm 14:1

AT **EMORY UNIVERSITY** in Atlanta, Georgia, in 1963, Paul van Buren declared that "the word 'God' is dead."[1] The prestigious southern learning institution became the grave plot where God had been laid to rest. The denial of God's existence is an atrocious, ludicrous and offensive assertion for devoted followers of the Christian faith, but to a world that has eaten at the tables of Altizer, Freud, Hegel, Blake, and Harvey Cox, and has been bombarded by a pervasive media that is almost exclusively atheistic or agnostic, this denial has become law. For you and me, history is linear: It has a beginning and end. For most of our culture, it is evolutionary, left to happenstance and chance, the dynamics of societal and physical lottery. A Dutch philosopher, Herman Dooyeweerd, described history in these terms:

> History has no windows looking out into eternity. Man is com-
> pletely enclosed in it and cannot elevate himself to a supra-
> historical level of contemplation. History is the be-all and end-all
> of man's existence and of his faculty of experience.[2]

We live in a world that is pregnant with the "there is no God" philosophy. There are no absolutes; morality is a personal and situational issue. Although the Church is outnumbered, although there are plenty of "fools" saying "there is no God," I want to remind us of Henry David Thoreau's comforting assessment: "Any man more right than his neighbors is a majority of one."[3] We serve a faithful God in the midst of a planet populated by foolish hearts.

The fool is the person who denies that God exists. Such people live their lives independent of any creator, any revelation, any set of moral and ethical guidelines. They operate without restriction.

Probably the first thing we think of when we hear the word *foolishness* is a diminished intellect. Psalm 111:10 provides the primary test of intellectual capacity: "The fear of the LORD is the beginning of wisdom; all who follow his precepts have good understanding. To him belongs eternal praise." Those who do not believe in God are, as my mother-in-law so colorfully puts it, "dumb as a clam." To deny God's existence is irrational, but it is a prevailing mindset in today's world. How else could we explain such blatant and "stick your tongue out" responses to Christian teaching and lifestyles? The fool lives for the moment, not for eternity.

Someone has described an atheist as a person "having no invisible means of support." Those who operate independently of God, who ignore Him or fail to acknowledge His existence or control, develop the moral fragrance of a garbage dump. Their lives are repulsive, their ethics animal-like. Love turns to lust, loyalty to adultery and generosity to greed. The milk has soured.

Without the road map, without the manual we call God's Word, without the Holy Spirit as pilot, modern man is bewildered and traveling at high gear in no direction. Many of us have lost our way and have not consulted the compass. The fog is heavy, the highways are unmarked and the hazards are many. Isaiah 53:6 reminds us that everyone is at one time a lost traveler: "We all, like sheep, have gone astray, each of us has turned to our own way; and the LORD has laid on him the iniquity of us all." But fools refuse to be found, so they are at the mercy of a wicked world and do not have the assistance of a heavenly Father to watch over them. They need to come home!

These foolish hearts have an appetite to devour the people of God. We are in spiritual warfare. There is a conspiracy of

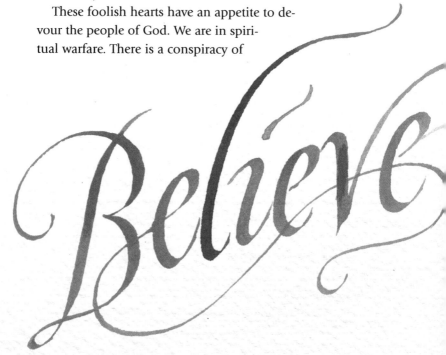

evil to confound the Christian agenda, confuse the Christian message and confine Christian people. We are a target, which makes the pagans of our culture salivate! Jesus clearly defined the antagonism that awaits us: "I have given them your word and the world has hated them, for they are not of the world any more than I am of the world" (John 17:14).

These foolish hearts are "overwhelmed with dread" (v. 5). The Hebrew for this description is "they feared a fear." Fools come to places of insecurity and uncertainty. Without a theology or a personal relationship with Jesus Christ, they fight their fears alone. They break into cold sweats! The boastful person has become the bawling child. The tough types have become squirming mice. Somewhere, sometime, the fool needs more than human resources—but their access is cut off, the supply beyond their reach. They need God, but they have separated themselves from Him. What a pathetic end!

I remember my mother referring to the three Rs, reading, 'riting and 'rithmetic. There are three Rs that adorn the end of this psalm, that lift up our heads and fill our hearts with renewed joy: refuge (v. 6), restoration (v. 7) and rejoicing (v. 7). They portray the benefits of a vital relationship with our God. We have a hiding place in Him, a hospital where the Chief of Staff can heal us of any deformity or infirmity, and a river of joy that is always flowing with promise!

The foolish hold in their hands a bunch of puzzle parts that will never fit together. We hold in our hearts the Holy Spirit of God, who created the puzzle in the first place.

Our worldview is a theocratic one. Our God is in control. Our Jesus has come and demonstrated His authority over the physical, natural and demonic forces that operate within our sphere of existence. We cry out, "Thus saith the Lord!" We shout, "Jesus is the Lord of history!" We minister in the power of God, who enables us to stand tall in a collapsing world.

Compelling Thought

The answer to the question, "Do I believe in God?" also answers the question, "What is the IQ of my heart?"

Comforting Prayer

Dear Lord and my God,

I submit to You that my desire is to have a wise heart. I want You to be the center of my life. Reveal Yourself to me again and again, through the world around me, the Word before me and the Holy Spirit within me. May my lips and life demonstrate my determined commitment to follow Jesus Christ, Your Son and my Shepherd.

PSALM 19

Knowing God through Sky and Scripture

> The heavens declare the glory of God;
>> the skies proclaim the work of his hands.
>>> Psalm 19:1

> The law of the Lord is perfect,
>> refreshing the soul.
> The statutes of the Lord are trustworthy,
>> making wise the simple.
>>> Psalm 19:7

THE CHRISTIAN FAITH is born in the womb of revelation. Had God chosen to hide Himself, we would never have found Him. God has chosen, however, to reveal Himself, and this psalm of David focuses on two of the primary ways that we can see and know our heavenly Father.

This capsule on God's revealing nature is built on two components, the skies and the Scriptures. What God has created and what God has written serve to disclose the divine Person and plan. This revelatory hymn moves us to the telescope as we look at the canopy of the constellations, and then it bids us to reach for the microscope as we view the words of Holy Scripture and pan for their glorious gold.

The stars are God's oldest witnesses. They are a silent, shining tribute to His handiwork. Verse one is a classic case of Hebrew parallelism, where the same idea is stated in similar ways. The "heavens" and the "skies" are basically the same entity. This redundancy reinforces the psalmist's point: "Look at the sky and you will increase your perception of God Almighty!" Jean Bon St. Andre, during the French Revolution, said to a believing peasant, "I will have all your steeples pulled down, that you may no longer have any object by which you may be reminded of your old superstitions." "But," replied the peasant, "you cannot help leaving us the stars."[1]

Natural revelation is present during the day and the night (v. 2). This perpetual festival never ends. These time/light designations of creation envelop us with God's presence. We may deny God, but we cannot escape God!

In my Father's world there is a single star we call the sun (vv. 4–6), which is an ambassador to all the earth. It is a solar cell of energy that races across the sky like a bridegroom coming out of his chamber. Every atom on earth is touched by its heat! It is a comprehensive messenger that is a bond slave to the God of the ages!

But there is a more precise revelation that is specific in revealing this Creator—it is the Scriptures, which define in particular who God is, and what course we humans should take to reach Him and live in His image.

The latter half of the psalm is a writer's dream for one who loves to alliterate! Verses 7–14 extol the Scriptures as revealing

KNOWING GOD THROUGH SKY AND Scripture

God and His intentions for individuals who want to live in spiritual wholeness and holiness.

This Lord is a Lawgiver (v. 7). The Scriptures serve to convert the sinner to a saint. The verb *convert* has the force of bringing back, like a shepherd's crook pulls in a wayward ewe. The testimony of God makes wise the simple! The dunce becomes the Delphi Oracle!

The scriptural statutes are right (v. 8). This leads to a rejoicing heart because our very lives are not grounded on the quicksand of speculation, but on the *terra firma* of God's infallible Word. Light dawns in the midst of heavy darkness, and we exclaim, "Once I was blind, but now I can see!" This is happy medicine from heaven, which cheers the convert.

The Scriptures change us, our goals, our aspirations, our values. Where once we craved gold, we now crave God. Where once we craved food, we crave faith. These Scriptures are more to be desired than gold and taste sweeter than honeycomb (v. 10).

The Scriptures reveal God's convicting nature: They put pressure on us to change. They corner us! They flash before us like a yellow warning light to signal danger. The servant is warned, and his obedience leads to great reward (v. 11). In reference to the Bible, someone has written, "Sin will keep me from this Book, or this Book will keep me from sin."

The Scriptures declare God's cleansing and forgiving nature (v. 12). At times our minds do misfire, and we commit foolish, stupid, unjustified sins. The Word is like the laver at the tabernacle, a polished metal bowl that held water; the worshiper could first see his or her blemish in its mirror-like surface, and then be cleansed by its waters. The Word reveals and then removes!

The Scriptures correct (v. 13). They make the downright upright, and the guilty innocent. They enhance our fellowship with others and our relationship with God. David's final prayer should be the goal for all of us—that the words of our mouths and meditations of our hearts be acceptable (v. 14). In general revelation and in special revelation, may we be inspired from above and instructed from within to stand in His holy presence unashamed.

Compelling Thought

The answer to the question, "Do I daily see God in the skies and in the Scriptures?" also answers the question, "Do I daily increase my knowledge of God?"

Comforting Prayer

Dear heavenly Father,
   I stand in Your art gallery every day of my life. I am amazed at Your creation as it speaks of Your power and majesty. I also travel through Your Word each day, and I praise You for its teaching and truth. Please continue to show Yourself to me through natural theology and through the treasures in Your written Word.

PSALM 22

Lift My Thoughts

My God, my God, why have you forsaken me?
Why are you so far from saving me, from the words
of my groaning?

Psalm 22:1 ESV

O PSALM is quoted more frequently in the New Testament than Psalm 22. It has been labeled "the psalm of the cross." Its original context addresses the disorientation and darkness of David's life. Its prophetic context wraps itself around the agony of Jesus Christ, who became sin for us and died on the cross. Many of the realities of this Old Testament psalm became painful facts for Jesus as He endured the cross for the sake of God's fallen creatures. David cries out in his powerful lament, "My God, my God, why have you forsaken me?" Jesus selected David's cry and made it His own as He was suspended between heaven and earth, as the blood congealed on His sacred skin, as the sweat rolled down His precious brow, as the people mocked and ridiculed His pathetic plight. God's Son spoke these words of loneliness and abandonment: "My God, my God, why have you forsaken me?" These are personal words, passionate words, piercing words, and they beg for an answer.

The answer is found in God's will. Sometimes His servants and His sons and daughters, and even His beloved, only begotten Son, experience hurt so that healing may come. God permits and allows despair, disdain and sometimes death to visit those He cherishes, in order to bring light and love and life.

David incorporates many expressions that describe the attack upon his body. As generations read the psalmist's descriptions, their minds have raced to the dear Savior, who, before His disciples "took bread, gave thanks and broke it, and gave it to them, saying, 'This is my body given for you; do this in remembrance of me'" (Luke 22:19). Long before Jesus came to earth, about one thousand years before our Lord's visit to our planet, David felt the brokenness of his own body. In verses 14 and 15, he presents a litany of excruciating torment. He depicts himself as "poured out like water"; his bones are twisted out of joint, his heart has melted like wax, his strength is dried up like a broken piece of earthenware that has baked in a Palestinian sun, his tongue sticks to the roof of his mouth as if it has been clamped there, and he claims to be lying in the dust of death. This great warrior has become a man tortured to the point of being a spectacle.

The imagery David selects to portray his attackers is stunning. His adversaries are raging bulls, roaring lions and wild dogs—and they have pierced his hands and feet. The reader of this psalm almost wants to ask him to stop talking about such devastating circumstances, like a mother at the supper table tells her children to cease talking about gory details that threaten to bring indigestion.

We must move the video forward to Jesus, as the gospel writers did when they became journalists describing the agony of Jesus

Christ. The scribes and Pharisees were bullish in their attempts to discredit His miraculous ministry and halt His holy crusade. So many segments of the wicked were engaged in plotting against Him. His hands and feet were pierced, His tongue was glued to His beautiful mouth, and He confessed His dryness with the exclamation, "I thirst" (John 19:28 ESV). The garments that covered His body were removed, and gamblers cast lots for the Savior's humble wardrobe.

Both David and Jesus tasted the bitterness of suffering; their bodies screamed with lacerating pain, and the heavenly Father withheld His hand so that greater good would be attained. The great king of Israel and the King of kings both groaned as their bodies were broken by the evil conspiracies of wicked men and because of the permissive will of God. For David, his brokenness would be answered with God's saving right hand; for Jesus, His brokenness would lead to the salvation of mankind.

David employed a very pitiful word picture to describe himself in Psalm 22:6: "I am a worm and not a man, scorned by men and despised by the people" (EHV). The Hebrew word for "worm" is also used to describe the crimson crocus from which scarlet stain was obtained to color the robes of kings. This may well be a reference to the shedding of Jesus' blood. I can remember as a child watching worms as they innocently traveled on my sidewalks, and in my younger days I relished catching up to them and squashing them until their blood burst out. Jesus' blood spilled like that of the worm as He sacrificed Himself so that you and I would not have to be punished for our sins.

Certainly, the piercing of the hands and feet that David explicitly mentions in verse 16 describes the blood he shed in the hour of his despair. Jesus would also spill His blood on His journey to Calvary, and He shed it freely on the cross. Isaiah would prophesy of the Messiah's piercing with these words: "But he [Jesus] was pierced for our transgressions" (53:5). The blood of Jesus was poured out, not because He had any sin, stain or impediment, but to satisfy the requirement that was needed for the forgiveness of our failures.

Our spiritual ancestor David did not enjoy his suffering. And, as we listen in on Jesus' conversation with His heavenly Father, we clearly comprehend the dreadful nature of the suffering that He was to endure, and from which He asked to escape: "My Father, if it is possible, may this cup be taken from me. Yet not as I will, but as you will" (Matthew 26:39). Jesus desired to bypass the cup of suffering—so much so that He asked the Father two more times to forego it (Matthew 26:42, 44). Yet He submitted Himself to the Father's perfect yet painful plan.

Psalm 22 ends well. David proceeds to declare God's deliverance and reign over circumstances and nations. It is noteworthy that his final words are "He has done it" (22:31), which in Hebrew is one word, *asah*, which means "finished." In similar fashion, when Jesus is on the threshold of death on the cross, He uses one Greek word, *tetelestai*, which means "finished" (John 19:30).

This prophetic psalm speaks to us, indeed, shouts to us that God has decisively dealt with our trauma and our transgressions. Our lament, like David's, has been transformed into a song of thanksgiving. A broken body and the shedding of blood has ended at salvation! The broken have been blessed, the forsaken have been fortified, the hurting have been healed! Isn't that just like God? He turns thorns into thrones and crosses into crowns.

Compelling Thought

The answer to the question, "Why did David and Jesus suffer?" also answers the question, "Why do the righteous suffer?"

Comforting Prayer

Dear Lord,

Though my suffering does not approach the intensity of David's or Yours, Lord Jesus, I still have my moments of grief and disappointment that cast a shadow over my day. Make me strong in the darker days of my journey and lift my thoughts to the reality that the sun is always beyond the thunder clouds of my life.

Day 7

PSALM 23

My Shepherd

The LORD is my shepherd; I shall not want.

Psalm 23:1 NKJV

THE SURVIVAL OF SHEEP is absolutely dependent upon shepherds. Sheep are not intelligent, are prone to wander, have no defense system, are afraid of water and rank as perhaps the most helpless animal that grazes. Sheep that have a good shepherd are guaranteed a happy existence, because it is the shepherd who sets the quality of life for those he or she tends.

Scripture portrays God's children as sheep; the metaphor appears in both the Old and the New Testaments. Perhaps no other piece of literature in the world so beautifully portrays this analogy as Psalm 23. This is the cornerstone of David's writings. The message is calm and confident. It transcends the vicissitudes of life and ends with the sheep being brought home. The psalm has been used to lead people into the inner chambers of the Kingdom. It has been employed as therapy for those who fear and fret. It is verbalized in the nursery to pacify a young mother who holds a bleating baby and wonders how this vulnerable creature will ever endure the chilly winds of this world. These words are often shared in the intensive care unit when the patient senses that the doctor has done the maximum and there are no more options and no more alternatives. It is most frequently found in the funeral service because it treats death not as a house we will dwell in, but a porch we will step off of into a new and better world.

If an animals' Gallup Poll of favorite sermons could be taken, I believe that the sheep would rate Psalm 23 as their favorite homily, with verse one serving as the title. There is no panic in this song from the heart of David, one of God's sheep. There is promise and peace and a composure that people dream about. This is no illusion! If you have accepted God's love and forgiveness, you have a Shepherd who charts your tomorrows and provides in miraculous and eternal ways.

As humans have defined themselves with existentialism and humanism, they have moved away from God. David embraced the Father God and made certain that those who read his writings understood that he was singular in his choice. He deployed a singular article as he opened the psalm, which narrows the field to one Lord. His choice for describing this God or Lord is the word *Yahweh*, the label that God chose when He introduced Himself to Moses. A broad definition of this title would be: "I-am-becoming-everything-you-need is my Shepherd."

What an incredible description for a shepherd! This keeper of the sheep has inexhaustible resources and can satisfy abundantly every demand the sheep would ever have. If we all could realize and believe in God's absolute ability to fill the bill whatever the crisis, whatever the circumstances, what a bright world this would be! Watch people as they try to "do it themselves," or as they turn to some other limited human to resolve their dilemma, or as they hope for "Lady Luck" to be the winning difference in their lives. Is it any wonder that this world's inhabitants seem to be in so much turmoil? David, with the softness of Indian silk, states, "The Lord is my Shepherd."

The analogy of shepherd came out of David's own lifestyle. David's biography in Scripture portrays him, in his early years, as an admirable shepherd. He even stood as savior for his sheep against the likes of a lion and a bear—that is beyond the call of duty! But with all of David's admirable skill and understanding of shepherding, we can appreciate this analogy even more than the writer, for we are witnesses of the Chief Shepherd, Jesus Christ.

The New Testament portrays three situations where Jesus functioned as a shepherd toward His sheep. These scriptural scenarios reveal the shepherd acting in three ways: First, the shepherd sees his sheep; second, the shepherd seeks his sheep; third, the shepherd sacrifices himself for his sheep in order to save them. As we study Jesus, the meaning of the psalm swells like a sponge tossed in a bucket of water. "The Lord is my shepherd" becomes pregnant with powerful new meaning!

In Matthew 9, Jesus is blitzing the countryside, preaching and teaching, healing every disease and infirmity, and His fame is spreading like a forest fire. In the midst of this campaign, He looks around, and His eyes focus on the people and their desperate plight. Matthew 9:36 states, "But when he saw the multitudes, he was moved with compassion on them, because they fainted, and were scattered abroad, as sheep having no shepherd" (KJV). This Shepherd has a watchful eye gazing on His sheep, and even when they are scattered across the valleys and mountains of this world, His eye is still observing them, and not only registering their plight but being moved by their pain and confusion.

my Shepherd

In Luke 15, Jesus has mingled with the tax collectors and sinners, the social outcasts and deviants of that day. The Pharisees slam Him for His company, and then follows His parable of the "ninety and nine." A shepherd with a flock of a hundred sheep discovers that one is missing. In our contemporary era, majority rule and bottom-line thinking would have dictated that the shepherd ignore this one sheep and concentrate on the remaining flock. I must confess that this approach makes sense to me. As the parable unravels, however, the shepherd sets out to find this stray, and he leaves behind the entire flock to save one solitary sheep. He retrieves this lost lamb, assumes the lamb's burden on his shoulders, probably because this sheep couldn't even walk home, and then calls his friends and neighbors to rejoice with him over the reclamation of this single sheep. We have a Shepherd who seeks.

In John 10, Jesus gives commentary on His role as shepherd. It is an astonishing profile of His love, which stretches even into the dark corridors of death. Four times in this passage, Jesus speaks of death as essential to the Good Shepherd's role. He distinguishes the shepherd from the hireling who only stays by the sheep until the wolf comes, and then takes his money and races away. Jesus tells us that the sheep He cares for find life! Most shepherds raise sheep for one reason, to make a profit and eventually to slaughter the sheep. This Shepherd changes places because of His love—the sheep live and He forfeits *His* life!

The little word "my" in verse one makes this psalm up close and personal. There is no swallowing up of our identity by large numbers of sheep. This one-to-one relationship has such an amazing therapeutic value to our sanity and security when we realize we are Jesus Christ's personal pet project.

If Jesus is not who He said He is, then we sheep can count on the slaughter; we might as well start our pathetic bleating and begin our slow and steady procession to the slaughterhouse. But if He is the Good Shepherd and can deliver what He promised, then we are in good hands and our manifest destiny is this: "Surely goodness and mercy shall follow me all the days of my life; and I will dwell in the house of the LORD forever" (v. 6 NKJV). The sheep smile today, because they know their Shepherd is already preparing for tomorrow!

Compelling Thought

The answer to the question, "Who is my shepherd?" also answers the question, "Will I have everything I need?"

Comforting Prayer

Dear Shepherd,

My gratitude cannot be expressed in any language for the ministry that You invest in my life. I am so lost and bewildered without You. Keep me close to You, that I may experience the incredible benefits of following You.

PSALM 23

Quiet Waters and Green Pastures

He makes me lie down in green pastures;
He leads me beside quiet waters.
He restores my soul;
He guides me in the paths of righteousness
For His name's sake.

Psalm 23:2–3 NASB1995

S WE OBSERVED IN DAY 7, Psalm 23 opens with a grand affirmation: "The LORD is my shepherd, I shall not want" (NASB1995). The rest of the psalm details why the sheep is so ecstatic about the shepherd. The remainder of the psalm forms the diary of a sheep, with personal observations about the one who watches over it.

The entries of this diary are best understood by realizing that sheep possess many liabilities. Chief among them are: (1) they are resistant to lying down; (2) they are horrified by running water;

(3) they have difficulty restoring themselves to their feet if they are rolled over; (4) they walk habitually in the same paths, destroying forage and forming ruts.

In the late-morning environment of the East, the sheep face a scorching, sizzling, searing sun. They need to lie down and be still. Sheep, however, obstinately refuse to take this therapeutic action because of their compelling fears. They fear their enemies; lying down makes them vulnerable to wolves and other predators. They fear the other sheep; they want to avoid becoming susceptible to attack from within. They fear that petty flies and parasites may annoy them. And finally, they fear going hungry; an empty stomach keeps them on their feet grazing.

The problem is that if they do not rest in the midst of these fears, they will eventually be destroyed by exhaustion and fatigue. The good shepherd allays their fears and seeks to satisfy their needs so that the sheep assume this vital rest position. In this frantic age in which we live, we sheep are also resistant to lying down, to resting and being refreshed in God's love and providence. There must be parentheses and pauses in our lives. Vance Havner pointed out that what Jesus said, "'Come ye yourselves apart . . . , and rest a while' (Mark 6:31) is a must for every Christian. If you don't come apart, you will come apart!"[1] The contemporary sheep must believe in the shepherd's ability to deal with the hostile world that surrounds him. They must trust in the shepherd's ability to watch while they recline.

Where does the shepherd lay his sheep down? The answer is crucial to our concept of the Good Shepherd. He places us in green pastures. Green pastures satisfy the ewes' need to produce heavy milk flow. Also, in lush, green pastures, sheep fill up quickly and therefore lie down sooner. Finally, green pastures prevent the animals from becoming scrawny and sickly sheep, caused by long searches for rare patches of green grass in a desolate terrain. Sheep are prone to choose inferior pastures. The shepherd, however, expends great energy to discover the prime pastures that will serve his sheep most abundantly.

Years ago I was mother and father to our oldest son, Matthew, while his mother was away. It was my responsibility to prepare the place where he would lie down. My "little sheep" was quite distressed when he walked in and found that the "shepherd" had not made the bed, and that Mickey Mouse and Hug-a-Bunny were not placed in proper position. You see, I didn't want to be bothered with mattress covers, sheets and blankets. I didn't want to fluff pillows and position special partners. But I understand that in order for my sheep to sleep, he wants everything orderly, wrinkle-free and placed in position. In like manner, God understands His sheep. And I am told that shepherds must sometimes develop their pasture, which means clearing, plowing, tearing out, seeding, irrigating and husbanding the grass. My Shepherd has gone to great lengths to ensure that where I lie down is redemptive and restful to me.

Sheep fear running water. The shepherd must find those still pools that will allow the flock to quench their thirst and replenish their water supply. The answer to why sheep fear turbulent water is found in their thick wool. They are pitifully poor swimmers because their coats absorb the water and make them a deadweight. It would be similar to us trying to swim with a waterlogged winter coat.

The Good Shepherd knows our weaknesses. He has a way of compensating for them. He provides ways and means by which our essential needs are met, and not at the expense of our own well-being. In our spiritual journey, there are tempestuous times that prevent us from being nourished and strengthened. It is the

Shepherd who leads us into the quiet valleys and who bids us come to the tranquil pools of the prayer closet, the devotional study of the Bible, the soothing Christian book, the sharing of thoughts with a Christian friend, the glimpse of a quiet sunset, the musing of time and eternity under a starlit sky. God provides those special pools of promise and peace, without which we sheep would soon dry up and dehydrate our spiritual supply!

It was Augustine who contended that soul rest only occurs when we rest in our Creator.[2] It was Tolstoy who spoke of man's thirst for God. It was Pascal who contended in our vernacular, there is a hole in every man's soul and only God can fill it![3] The rest is found, the thirst is satisfied, the vacuum is filled by God's presence and power, and the person of His Holy Spirit. We need to exercise our option of turning away from a world in turmoil, from the tyranny of the urgent, to those streams that slowly filter in the deserts of this world, to those pools of holy presence.

The old English term "cast down" describes sheep that have turned over on their backs, with feet projected heavenward. They are often unable to restore themselves to an upright position. When we do a spiritual "belly-up," we have a Shepherd who can restore us to our feet. Our sheeply tendencies lead us to roll over sometimes, but the Lord Jesus, being the Good Shepherd that He is, bends down to our difficulty and applies His strength to get us vertical again. Jesus is combing the fields of this world, watching for "cast down" sheep. He is able to deliver us from our belly-up times if we will allow Him to come near us.

In the East, shepherds always go ahead of their flocks, because sheep have an overwhelming Achilles' heel in their portfolio— they habitually get lost! Isaiah 53:6 accentuates this weakness: "We all, like sheep, have gone astray, each of us has turned to [his] own way."

In contrast we have Jesus claiming, "I am the way, the truth, and the life" (John 14:6 NKJV). This is our steadfast hope—that our Shepherd is not leading us to a dead end, but in right paths so that eventually we can get home again!

We sheep need to leave the leading up to the Lord. Leadership depends on the ability to see ahead, to chart a course that in the long run is superior to all others. The shortsightedness of sheep, which can only see ten or fifteen yards in advance, leads them into perilous places. Our Shepherd stands taller and can see farther than we can. We must not judge God's paths until they are complete. What may appear to be the wrong direction, may in the long run be the way home.

F. B. Meyer put it this way: "Not always beside the gentle stream, but sometimes by the foaming torrent. Not always over the delicate grass, but sometimes up the stony mountain track. Not always in the sunshine, but sometimes through the valley of the shadow of death. But whichever way it is, it is the right way, and it leads home."[4]

Do you need rest? He makes me lie down!

Do you need freedom from your fears? He leads me beside the still waters!

Do you need to be made whole again? He restores my soul!

Do you need to be led to glorify Him? He leads me in the paths of life!

Compelling Thought

The answer to the question, "Whom am I following?" also answers the question, "Will my diary be a delight or a disaster?"

Comforting Prayer

Dear Shepherd,

There are many times when I give up on green pastures and still waters. Help me to look beyond the five senses to the faith reality that exists in and beyond this world. You know exactly where to lead Your sheep, so don't let me relish my independence. I don't want to walk in circles; lead me in Your path of righteousness, which ends in a glorious heaven!

PSALM 23

Lead Me Home

Even though I walk
    through the valley of the shadow of death,
I will fear no evil,
    for you are with me;
your rod and your staff,
    they comfort me.
You prepare a table before me
    in the presence of my enemies;
You anoint my head with oil;
    my cup overflows.
Surely goodness and mercy shall follow me
    all the days of my life,
and I shall dwell in the house of the LORD
    forever.

Psalm 23:4–6 ESV

S WE LOOK OVER David's shoulder, we notice a change in his diary. There is a shift in his references to the Shepherd from the third-person pronoun, *He*, to the second-person pronoun, *You*. There is an

LEAD ME HOME

intimacy, a closeness that seems to draw the Shepherd and the sheep to each other in the final entries. Our sheep is going to describe enemies and the final enemy, death, and yet his constant confidence in the ability of the Shepherd to bring him home is not diminished. Sheep do wander, but this particular sheep knew his final destiny: "I shall dwell in the house of the LORD forever" (ESV)!

There is now a new urgency, a critical test for the sheep and his Keeper. The valley of the shadow of death poses a monumental test as the sheep makes his journey to the sheepfold. It is a part of every sheep's path, and it is essential that the Shepherd overcome this perilous place!

Several observations leap out from the diary. The landscape darkens in this valley of death. The sheep no longer runs or frolics; he is slowed to a walk. The terrain is not clearly seen, and the dangers are not clearly known. It is the Shepherd's vision that must compensate for the impoverished vision of the sheep.

Why can you have confidence in your Shepherd when you travel through such a frightening place? First, Psalm 139:12 teaches you this truth about the Lord: "The darkness and the light are both alike to Thee" (KJ21). The brightness or the dimness of our paths does not affect our Shepherd's vision in the least. He is not handicapped by the amount of light!

Second, the Shepherd has traveled this path before and knows each step His sheep should take. Our Good Shepherd pioneered a path through this valley when He was crucified and entered through death's domain. The old hymn "My Lord Knows the Way through the Wilderness" tells us that because He knows the way already, we sheep only have to follow Him. He has diluted the punch of this dark and foreboding valley.

Third, the Shepherd knows that this is the way home. Death is the gateway to life! When our family traveled home from western Pennsylvania and northern Indiana, we had to come through the tunnels on the Pennsylvania Turnpike. Our children were aware that we were moving into darkness and would wonder what was happening. Faye and I would reassure them that this was a part of going home, and soon they saw light!

The word "shadow" is crucial to an understanding of this psalm. A shadow is not the real thing! A shadow pretends to be reality, but it cannot function as the real McCoy. A dog's shadow cannot bite; a tree's shadow cannot fall and hurt you. And death's shadow cannot destroy you, because Jesus Christ met and defeated the substance of death. We only encounter the shadow! According to the sheep writing this psalm, the valley of death has lost its terror.

One more essential point needs to be made concerning shadows: There must be light for a shadow to exist. There is no darkness too deep to keep the Good Shepherd from lighting the way.

The sheep sees two instruments—the rod and the staff—as consoling friends. The first was a heavy, hard club, two feet in length, which served as a defensive weapon to ward off predators. Another use of the rod was to count the sheep.

The eight-foot staff was employed to discipline sheep, but also to hook them back from danger. The shepherd's crook has salvaged millions of sheep from falling from great heights or drowning in deep waters. The crook becomes a life buoy!

The staff was also used for digging. The shepherd "prepared a table" for his sheep by going ahead of the flock and rooting out the poisonous shrubs and thorny plants that inhabited the sheep's tableland. The staff became a vital weapon in the shepherd's arsenal as he engineered the sheep's survival.

David could look back at the first communion service, which was held in Egypt the night the death angel swept over the land and touched the firstborn of every Egyptian household. On that night in an enemy land, the Israelites sat at a table and a lamb was eaten, a sacrificial animal that provided food and redemption from Pharaoh's henchmen. Today we look over our shoulder at the Lord's Supper, which found Jesus eating a religious meal "in the presence of [His] enemies." This became a memorial feast for us that we celebrate, commemorating Jesus' conquest of our enemies, even that most stubborn enemy, death. Jesus has weeded out the opposition and prepared a table of mercy and grace where we may feast at any given moment! We may be surrounded by our foes, but their cause is lost, and the war is won!

When the sheep pass a shepherd at night, he or she is sensitive to their need for anointing. There are many parasites that find their homes in a sheep's head. Sheep are so tortured by these parasites that they rub their heads against hard objects such as trees, rocks and posts. The sheep's system is so bothered that it often goes into hysteria trying to get relief. At the first sign of the infestation, the shepherd starts applying oil to the sheep's head, which serves to soothe the wounds and to prevent further flies from infecting the sheep.

Sheep get very thirsty in the arid climates of Palestine. Human sheep get very thirsty in the hostile climate of this world. David often had watered his sheep with an overflowing jug of water. The sheep's thirst was appeased. The sheep's need was satisfied. Jesus said, "Those who hunger and thirst for righteousness . . . will be filled" (Matthew 5:6 csb). We don't need to fear dehydration if we are close to our Shepherd.

This diary ends on the most encouraging note: We make it home. In a world like ours, where everything is unstable, where the only thing you can depend on is that nothing can be depended on, in this kind of fluctuating world, we long for permanence. We grasp for eternity, and in this psalm, we hear eternity's whisper. The sheep's ears are eager to hear the Shepherd's song, "It won't be long until My steps will lead you home."

The Shepherd leads the sheep, and goodness and mercy follow Him. F. B. Meyer called goodness and mercy the "celestial escort."[1] Charles Spurgeon called them "God's footmen,"[2] alluding to the two men who took their place behind the coach in his day. They jumped out to open the door when the coach stopped. They ran ahead into inns to prepare the rooms. They made the journey smooth!

We sheep scare easily, but the Shepherd is always there and will lead us home! This beautiful psalm has given peace to the pilgrim for over twenty-five centuries! It still means as much, maybe more, than it meant to David on the Palestinian plain that supported his sheep. It lives for you today.

Compelling Thought

The answer to the question, "Will the Good Shepherd walk with me through the valley of the shadow of death?" also answers the question, "Will I be full of fear or faith when I walk through it?"

Comforting Prayer

Dear Lord Jesus,

You are the Shepherd I need to navigate me through life. Increase my faith in You, so that when my time comes to walk through the valley of the shadow, I will be strong and courageous, knowing that You have led me all the way and that You can lead me through that day of darkness into glorious light!

Day 10

PSALM 25

Master Teacher

Show me your ways, LORD,
   teach me your paths.
Guide me in your truth and teach me,
   for you are God my Savior,
   and my hope is in you all day long.

Psalm 25:4–5

AVID IS IN JEOPARDY. His circumstances are life-threatening. In this psalm he briefs the reader with a description of his dilemma. He is a candidate to be shamed (vv. 2, 20); he needs forgiveness from his iniquity (v. 11); he feels like he's already caught in a snare (v. 15); he is lonely (16); and the number of his enemies is multiplying (v. 19). Abraham Lincoln's comment, "I have often been driven to God by the overwhelming sense that I had nowhere else to go,"[1] seems to fit David like a custom-made suit. Like a marathon runner in a blinding snowstorm, he is incapable of finding his way!

Why does our hero approach God? In this medium-sized passage of Scripture, David provides the rationale. The Lord has a reputation for great mercy (v. 6). A lost or wayward sheep is much better served by a compassionate shepherd than a cruel one. The expectation of the one praying is that God will remember him from the street corner of His love (v. 7), rather than from the scrapbook of David's sins (v. 7). Our faith must always look to the goodness of our Savior rather than to the guilt of our many sins. Those who major on their bleak past put a lid on their unwritten future. David's hope (vv. 3, 5, 21) is riveted not only to mercy and love but to God's goodness (v. 7), His faithfulness (v. 10), His name (v. 11) and His marvelous grace (v. 16)—that is, His propensity to give us what we don't deserve. Our appeals

MASTER TEACHER

must pass through the friendly confines of God's attributes, not the mine fields of our past mistakes. Our spiritual ancestor had the discernment to approach God regarding His difficulties on the basis of divine character, not human failure.

Though David requests deliverance from sin and his opponents, the most recurrent theme in this psalm of petitions resides in the author's passionate desire to be led by the quintessential teacher, by the ultimate scholar. We identify with David as his personal instincts and experience are insufficient to function as a dependable instrument panel. The relentless pursuit of God's way prompts David to engage in a semantic smorgasbord of terms to communicate to the Lord his desperate demands to be shown the way: "show me" (v. 4), "guide me" (v. 5), "teach me" (v. 5) and his assessment that the Master Teacher "instructs sinners" (v. 8), as well as "guides and teaches" the humble His way (v. 9).

Will the Lord respond favorably to the urgent cries of His child? Again, David provides the answers in his text. The humble (v. 9), the obedient (v. 10) and those who fear the Lord (v. 14) can be confident that the questions of the searching head will be met by the answers of a heavenly heart! Why not approach the Lord and allow Him to use His impeccable instrument panel to pilot your life onto His runways?

Compelling Thought

The answer to the question, "Who is my teacher?" also answers the question, "Is the course worth it?"

Comforting Prayer

Dear Lord,

I am ready to learn from the Master Teacher. Without You I will fumble and fail, but with You I believe I can pass life's course with flying colors. Please show me, guide me and teach me. I seek to honor You and be an honor student for You.

PSALM 30

Exalt the Lord

> I will exalt you, LORD,
> > for you lifted me out of the depths
> > and did not let my enemies gloat over me.
>
> Psalm 30:1

ALL OF US WORSHIP! We will all worship something or someone. It is both true and tragic that the majority of the members of our race have bowed down to other gods. The words of Hosea 8:4 have a painful and familiar ring: "With their silver and gold they make idols for themselves to their own destruction." Where is our allegiance? What is our level of commitment? Upon whom or what do we spend our time, talents and treasure?

Traditionally, when we hear the word "stewardship," we think of our purses and wallets, or credit cards and CDs. But proper teaching on stewardship appeals to a life totally lived for God, to His ultimate and majestic glory. God's people march to the beat of a different drummer. Our standards are higher, and our aims are

holier. We are not satisfied with the dusty lowlands of this world. You and I should be climbing higher—and in the process actually becoming a "living sacrifice," a goal that Paul characterized as "reasonable service," or the expected response (Romans 12:1 NKJV).

There is a danger in this type of emphasis. Some will say the call is too strong, the questions too personal, the cost too high. Yet God's expectation is a high road, a lofty ideal, an incredible adventure to be lived.

The author of Psalm 30 is David. The reason for its composition is debated, but the most convincing arguments suggest it was composed to be sung at the dedication of the temple. This beautiful passage later was incorporated into Jewish liturgy to commemorate the exile experience of Israel. Just prior to the time of Jesus Christ, it was employed at the celebration of Hanukkah, the feast that marks the rededication of the temple by Judas Maccabeus (165 BC) after its desecration by Antiochus Epiphanes just three years earlier. (This enemy of Judaism confiscated the holy vessels, captured the temple treasury, built a pagan altar on top of the holy altar and sacrificed swine upon it.) This psalm has tremendous historical overtones attached to it.

The application for us is extremely essential. Exalt God! Even when there is peril—praise Him! Even though there are enemies—exalt Him! Even though you may become content and self-confident, and because of that smugness end up in some kind of sticky dilemma—repent and serve Him as Lord! David is shouting through the centuries that God is the first Person of our lives and that our disposition is to be investing our lives for His glory, not our own. Why? For He alone turns wailing into dancing, and dark nights into joyful morning!

David knew the joy of victory and the agony of defeat. The rationale for his exaltation of his God is articulated in the initial verse of this psalm. "You lifted me out of the depths" is a watch-word woven throughout Old Testament poetry. The Hebrew word "lifted"[1] in its original meaning denotes the pulling up and down of buckets in a well. This God of Abraham, Isaac and Jacob had elevated him from distress to delight.

David had flirted with death and felt its icy breath, yet his extremity was met by God's opportunity, and he was delivered. David pledged himself to exalt God. It was a decision made of his volition: "I will exalt you, LORD." He made it a life principle to place God in the *numero uno* position—to give Him preeminence. His praise was built on a foundation of deliverance! Those who have reflected on the manifold mercies of God will be thankful people who cheerfully and willingly give their time, talents and treasures to Him.

David honors God in 30:5 for the contrast between His holy anger, which is momentary, and His divine favor, which stretches over a lifetime. You and I weep—David wept—but the weeping nights are countered by the rejoicing that comes in the morning.

I don't know about you, but for me, January and February are the night seasons of any year. Winter shortens the daylight, snow brings hazards to travel, nature has lost its wardrobe, and people see less of each other than at any other time. But what keeps me going is the realization that all things pass, for God has positioned spring to trail winter. Robins start congregating, trees start budding, and the air takes on a moist and fresh feel. This hope of spring is such a life buoy to the doldrums of the winter season.

It is interesting that the Hebrew word for "joy" can be used for the ringing cry of sorrow or joy! So we could say that to the extent that we lament our sorrows, God will compensate in full with laughter for our successes.

Thomas Brooks wrote a beautiful thought in Spurgeon's commentary on the Psalms:

> Their mourning shall last till morning. God will turn their winter's night into a summer's day, their sighing into singing, their grief into gladness, their mourning into music, their bitter into sweet, their wilderness into paradise.[2]

However, deliverance has within it the seeds of destruction. David confesses his smugness, perhaps even cockiness or arrogance, as he remarks, "I will never be shaken" (v. 7 TLV). The "comfort zone" is dangerous territory. Just because you stand somewhere, doesn't mean you can't fall, warns Paul in the New Testament (1 Corinthians 10:12). John Phillips made this observation: "As soon as things go our way we tend to become careless of spiritual things."[3] Spurgeon cautioned, "Few of us can bear unmingled prosperity."[4]

Our favor, firmness and faith are directly proportionate to our relationship with God and our dependence on Him. When we start talking self-reliance, rather than reliance on Him, we are an "accident waiting to happen." When we turn our back on God, it won't be long until we are flat on our back!

David found himself in a number of jams. We are not sure which "jam" he is referring to in Psalm 30, but it must have been a humdinger. We are fairly certain he contributed to its severity. With Hebrew parallelism in great supply, he inquires of God, "Is it better for me to die? And if I do, who will praise You—will the dust?" David resorts to a plea of desperation—he cries, "Help!"

David's enthusiasm for God can be traced to the Almighty's ability to turn the worst to the best, to step into our lives and make a welcome, wonderful exchange. There is a rainbow after the rain. The wailing is turned into dancing. The sackcloth, or mourning clothes, have been removed, and joy is draped over David's heart. This is a message we need to remember: It ain't over till God says it's over!

David's heart would not be silent. He exalted God—and though he never lived to see the temple, which this psalm was probably used to dedicate, his penchant for praise outlived that legacy of stone and wood.

Compelling Thought

The answer to the question, "How soon will I exalt the Lord and trust in His mercy?" also answers the question, "How long will I stay in the depths of despair?"

Comforting Prayer

Dear Lord,

You are my Helper and Healer. Remind me that my independence will only lead to sorrow, and my dependence on You will always lead to joy! I pledge to exalt You and to sing of Your love forever.

PSALM 32

Songs for the Forgiven

Blessed is the one
  whose transgressions are forgiven,
  whose sins are covered.
Blessed is the one
  whose sin the LORD does not count against them
  and in whose spirit is no deceit.

Psalm 32:1–2

THIS PSALM BEGINS AS IT ENDS—in joyful, jubilant song. Not since Psalm 1 has David begun one of his hymns with a "Blessed." There is so much triumph as Psalm 32 opens its front door to us. It is not the song of a self-righteous Pharisee, but of a pitiful publican. It is not the music of an elder brother who has pleaded his merits, but the melody of a maligned prodigal son who has proclaimed his despair and found deliverance. The publican has been justified; the prodigal son is eating prime rib with his regal robe around him and his flashing ring gleaming in the sunlight!

There are three striking words that pave the way for delirious rejoicing in the heart of David. The first word, *forgiven*, is a song in the night season. "Forgiven" means "to take off, to take away and to carry out of sight." That which was detestable, despicable and disgusting is no longer present. The filthy rags of Isaiah 64:6 are carted away by God's laundryman, and a new robe of righteousness is wrapped around the naked man. "Forgiven" is one of the sweetest-sounding words in our vocabulary, and in this psalm the uptight man becomes upright when he experiences it!

The second word is *covered*. Sin can be covered. Sin is like a scarlet stain, deeply embedded in the fabric of our souls. Men and women have cosmetically dealt with the stain of sin, but it seems to always wear its way through our camouflage. The grace of God has been distributed through the blood of a sacrificial lamb. The symbol of life has been recognized by God as a suitable covering for the sin-blemished soul. David had experienced the scarlet stains being made whiter than new-fallen snow!

The third word is *count*. Our sins are no longer recorded on our record! The person is guilty, but the record is destroyed. There is no penalty because there is no record. The festival of praise is triggered in verses 1 and 2 because the guilty is innocent, the pauper is now a prince, the sentenced sinner has now been declared a saint!

Sin can shame a singer to silence. The songs of silence are devastating in the hymnbook of our lives when there is transgression in our hearts. Confession is imperative—or pathetic living is imminent. David's portrait of the silent sinner is incredibly intense. His bones waxed old. There is a physical manifestation that results when a person feels guilty. The body seems to lose its vitality, energy and enthusiasm. Unconfessed sin often produces psychosomatic by-products. David says that God's hand of conviction is heavy upon him both night and day. There is no break, no

Songs for the forgiven

vacation and no intermission. The reminders of our transgressions seem to keep turning up like bad pennies. This is a loving function of our heavenly Father so that we will not continue with the cancer, but we will get the surgery. Our minds do not need to be tormented and harassed by sin, but if we are silent, time will provide no refuge. David uses the analogy of the almost-intolerable summer in Palestine, when temperatures soar upward, the wells go downward and dust chokes a man's palate. David seems to be choked by his silence; there is drought in his soul.

Verses 3 and 4 draw a pathetic picture of a soul unwilling to confess. There is no refreshment of the body, no rest for the mind, no relief for the soul. When believers clam up and praise diminishes to a trickle, there is just cause for lips to spring forth in confession, and then springtime will come. Dead churches are full of silent confessors!

Augustine said, "The beginning of understanding is to know thyself a sinner."[1] On a sunny day in Chicago in September 1972, a stern-faced, plainly dressed man could be seen standing on a street corner in the busy Chicago Loop. As pedestrians hurried by on their way to lunch or business, he would solemnly lift his right arm, and pointing to the person nearest him, intone loudly the single word "*GUILTY!*" Then, without any change of expression, he would resume his stiff stance for a few moments before repeating the gesture. Then, again, the man engaged in the inexorable raising of his arm, the pointing and the solemn pronouncing of the one word, "*GUILTY!*" The effect of this strange *j'accuse* pantomime on the passing strangers was extraordinary, almost eerie. They would stare at him, hesitate, look away, look at each other and then at him again, then hurriedly continue on their way. One man, turning to another (who was my informant), exclaimed, "But how did he know?" No doubt many others had similar thoughts. How did he know, indeed?

We know in our heart of hearts that there is a problem, but we are resistant to acknowledge our sin. David's awful agony over his sin was conquered only when he acknowledged it. Verse 5 is a beautiful expression of a man being freed from bondage: "I acknowledged my sin to you and did not cover up my iniquity. I said, 'I will confess my transgressions to the LORD.' And you forgave the guilt of my sin." David sent a telegram to God to report his transgression. So many of us have stopped sending telegrams to God; we are too reluctant to take care of our transgressions.

Confession is an arrow in the Christian's arsenal. David was not ashamed to admit that he slipped once in a while, that he stumbled along the way and that he depended on God to make things right. When the storm clouds are in the skies of your life, get into the ark of safety! And you will shout as David in verse 6, "Surely the rising of the mighty waters will not reach [me]." You will be able to say as David did in verse 7, "You are my hiding place." God does not shoot His wounded—He heals them!

The only time God speaks directly in Psalm 32 is in verses 8 and 9. It is as if He takes the microphone away from David and speaks to the audiences of the ages. His message is simple: You sinners can be students! He passionately tells us that He wants to direct our steps and lead us in wonderful ways. But we are often like horses and mules, which need bits and bridles to get them going in the right direction. God understands us, and He knows it is best to have our guilt removed and our sins taken away.

This psalm has a happy ending. There is gladness and rejoicing and shouting for joy! But remember, David acknowledged his sin prior to the party. We need to bring confession out of the Christian catacombs, dust it off and use it frequently in our faith. If you are on an empty tank and a gas station is right beside you, what should you do? If you are on an empty stomach and a full refrigerator is in the next room, what should you do? If your insulin level reaches the danger zone and the needle is lying on the table next to you, what should be your next step? If you are troubled and tentative in your faith because of some past act, some questionable thought, some unkind word, what should you do? You will not enjoy a season of thanksgiving until you have shared in the cleansing that follows confession. David was a great sinner, but also a great confessor. Are you singing and celebrating the riches of your God before a sad and sorry world? Let us lay aside every weight in our lives and the sins that keep us silent!

Compelling Thought

The answer to the question, "Why are you not praising God?" also answers the question, "When is the last time you confessed your sin?"

Comforting Prayer

Dear heavenly Father,

I choose to be a singer in my life and not a silent sinner. Please do the laundry in my life so that my heart may be pure and my song might be heard. Remove any sin, stain or impediment, and make my song a composition of praise and celebration to You!

PSALM 34

Endless Adoration

I will extol the LORD at all times;
his praise will always be on my lips.

Psalm 34:1

DAVID SETS BEFORE US one of the incredible goals for his life in Psalm 34:1—perpetual praise, or *praise that never quits.* This goal was the by-product of two monumental experiences in the young man's life in the land of Gath. The superscription tells us that this psalm of David was written when he changed his behavior before Abimelech, also known as Achish, king of Gath, and pretended that he was insane.

Imagine David's heart melting as he remembered his confrontation with Goliath of Gath. In this same land, he entered Israel's "Hall of Fame." It was here that, as the youngest of eight sons, he brought a snack to his brothers who were fighting the powerful Philistines. It was here that there came to his ears the sarcastic dares of a mammoth warrior who challenged any Hebrew to

ENDLESS ADORATION

match strength against him in a struggle to the death. It was on the soil of Gath where Goliath plummeted to the earth following David's bull's-eye to the giant's temple. It was here where Goliath's blood dripped to the dust after David retrieved the mighty soldier's sword and whacked off his head. Gath had been the land of conquest. It was easy to sing praise songs in that circumstance.

But David's victory led to perilous times. The best of times degenerated into the worst of times. Conquest became calamity! Saul, fearing the young upstart was a threat to his throne, began a series of attacks upon the shepherd boy's life. Two times Saul thrust his javelin at David. In a more subtle move, the king set him out in the battle's forefront, hoping to make him a heroic casualty. Eventually, David found himself a fugitive, harassed and hounded by Saul's army and on the king's "most wanted" list. These assaults drove David to the land of Gath, where he was discovered and his life hung in the balance before King Abimelech, whose nation still remembered the slaying of their legendary warrior, Goliath.

David found himself in severe straits. Realizing the desperation of the moment, the giant killer stooped to pretending he was a lunatic. The shepherd boy who did not fear Goliath feared Abimelech. The one who shook his fist at a giant was now making marks on the gates of the doors with his fingernails. The young man who verbally spat at Goliath's arrogance now allowed his spittle to drip down his beard and intensify his portrayal of a crazy man. Abimelech bought the performance and chased David out of Gath.

The sad scenario must have swept over David like a bitter November rain. His soul was soaked with the embarrassment of his cowardly choices. In the midst of his failure, a resolution was shaped in his soul: "I will extol the LORD at all times; his praise will always be on my lips." David engraved upon his heart what we must engrave upon ours. The weather may change, from sunshine to showers, but the weather in our hearts can be continually fair. If we really trust God, if He is really in control, then He is sovereign in both the day and the night seasons.

David's commitment in Psalm 34:1 rings with authority. "I will extol the LORD" is a steely statement of his posture toward life's peaks and pits. The will is involved in such a high plane of Christian living. This is an unconditional, unqualified posture of praise.

This quality of perpetual praise that David is talking about is found frequently in the Word. In Jonah 2:9 we read, "But I, with shouts of grateful praise, will sacrifice to you. What I have vowed I will make good. I will say, 'Salvation comes from the LORD.'" Submerged in a fish's belly, Jonah resolved to praise the Lord. Daniel responded to Darius's document, which would send him into the lions' den, by praising the Lord. "Now when Daniel learned that the decree had been published, he went home to his upstairs room where the windows opened toward Jerusalem. Three times a day he got down on his knees and prayed, giving thanks to his God, just as he had done before" (Daniel 6:10). Paul and Silas were singing at midnight in the Philippian jail, and the keeper of the prison found Jesus that night!

This attitude of perpetual praise is not an option in holy Scripture—it is a commandment. The New Testament plays this tune again and again. First Thessalonians 5:18 tells us to "Give thanks in all circumstances; for this is God's will for you in Christ Jesus." Listen to Paul in Philippians 4:6–7 (RSV):

> Have no anxiety about anything, but in everything by prayer and supplication with thanksgiving let your requests be made known to God. And the peace of God, which passes all understanding, will keep your hearts and your minds in Christ Jesus.

Praise leads to peace.

Hannah Whitall Smith said, "The soul that gives thanks can find comfort in everything; the soul that complains can find comfort in nothing."[1] One preacher said, "Praise is the lubrication that keeps your bearings from burning out!"

Compelling Thought

The answer to the question, "Do I praise God in stormy weather?" also answers the question, "Is my praise song perpetual or partial?"

Comforting Prayer

Dear heavenly Father,

I desire that my praise will not have a shelf life. Enable me, please, to manifest perpetual praise. Help me to have fair weather in my heart regardless of the circumstances that surround my life.

Day 14

PSALM 37

Do Not Fret

Do not fret because of those who are evil
or be envious of those who do wrong;
for like the grass they will soon wither,
like green plants they will soon die away.
Trust in the LORD and do good;
dwell in the land and enjoy safe pasture.

Psalm 37:1–3

AVID CONTRASTS the brief career of the wicked with the eternal inheritance of the righteous in this strategic psalm that helps the believer cope with the prosperity of those who do not serve God. Time is a crucial component of his argument, because time is on God's side. As we observe the "haves and have-nots," it does appear that the unbelieving definitely have an edge in the areas of leisure and possessions. We sometimes ask the Lord, "Why do those who dishonor You seem to do better in life than those who honor You?" The answer, according to Psalm 37, is, "It's just a matter of time!"

Three times David will present the injunction, "Do not fret." Two of the three instances cast the wicked in a very short-term position of success. The first verse of the psalm demands that the Christian take the "long view" of assessment. The wicked do prosper, but they are like grass that springs up quickly and soon withers away. The seventh verse also frames the success of the wicked in a very short-term scenario. Evil men do succeed for a season, but they will be cut off, a concept that occurs four other times in this psalm (vv. 22, 28, 34, 38).

The law of recurrence, when a word or idea occurs frequently in a document, demands that we take a serious look at this prediction and promise. Yes, the wicked prosper, but they do not inherit the land and possessions like the righteous. The law of recurrence operates on behalf of the righteous, for they are predicted and promised this reality of inheritance six different times (vv. 9, 11, 18, 22, 29, 34). The third time David challenges the believer not to fret is fascinating, because he does not catalog the situation of the wicked; rather, he states that if we persist in fretting about them, *we become like them*. In verse 8 he shows us the end of the journey when we fret—namely, we start to act evil. The wisdom of these "fret not" admonitions is so empowering when we realize that the wicked who flourish have such a short time to savor it.

In verses 3–6 David gives three counteractivities and their dividends during this temporary distortion that features unbelievers in an enviable position of success. First, verse 3 directs the believer to *trust in the Lord and do good*. Despite this apparent unfairness—the prosperity of the ungodly—the saints are to be tenacious about their trust in the Lord. And the lifestyle of the saints is to feature good deeds—holy deeds that manifest His will in wicked times. This translates into dwelling in the land with safe pasture.

When many readers encounter verse 4, they focus on the last half of it: "And he will give you the desires of your heart." What is so often forgotten is the initial half of this equation, which is our second counteraction: "*Delight [yourself] in the* LORD." As we engage and encounter the Lord, our joy levels escalate and we experience the ecstasy of His presence, which enables us to embrace His Word, His will and His way. Out of this personal relationship with the Lord, we come to want what He wants, and therefore His desires become our desires. And since His desires are fulfilled, we find the gratification of our desires because they were extrapolated from His mind and heart through our engagement with Him.

A third counteraction to keep us strong and stable in times like these is to *commit our way to the Lord*. The word *commit* in the

Hebrew means "to roll upon."[1] We can figuratively picture in our minds the rolling on to the Lord of our prayers, hopes and dreams, which seem in the short term to be sabotaged by the success of the wicked. Peter invites us in the New Testament to "Cast all your anxiety on him, because he cares for you" (1 Peter 5:7 EHV). This is a liberating exercise of faith in God.

Psalm 37 begins with an undesirable scenario; evil men are making a huge profit and having tremendous favor with their endeavors. But the psalm ends with the righteous being delivered from the wicked and possessing God as their refuge and stronghold. The believing heart must recognize that the unfaithful and unbelieving are like grass, which withers quickly, and like smoke, which vanishes away.

Over time, those who "do not fret" and who trust, delight and commit find themselves holding the deeds to all good and precious things. Wait patiently and do good deeds, and soon the time will come when the people of God receive their incredible inheritance through Jesus Christ, God's Son!

Compelling Thought

The answer to the question, "Do I fret much?" also answers the question, "How much do I trust in the Lord?"

Comforting Prayer

Dear Father,

Give me the eyes of faith that look at this world not just through the five senses but through biblical lenses that convert any situation into a win for You and Your children. Build into my inner man a steel-like confidence that tenaciously holds on to the principle that all things work together for good!

Day 15

PSALM 40

Wait Patiently

I waited patiently for the LORD;
he turned to me and heard my cry.

Psalm 40:1

SALM 40 DEALS FORCEFULLY with the issue of
waiting on God. If you are like me, you would rather
run than be on your knees. Waiting is anathema to my
fourth-gear, Type-A, hyperactive lifestyle. David was a
winner for God, but in this psalm he applauds the discipline of
waiting before winning. Scripture is sprinkled with those who ran
ahead of God, who jumped the gun and who were then shot by
that same gun. "To everything there is a season, a time for every
purpose under heaven" (Ecclesiastes 3:1 NKJV). This truth is for all
of us who have difficulty playing the waiting game.

The English text of Psalm 40:1 does not transmit the emphatic
statement of David relative to waiting. The Hebrew construction is
intense. A literal rendering would be, "Waiting, I waited."[1] If you go
back in your memory to the time you came home way late for your

mother's fine dinner, you might hear her say again, "I waited and waited and waited." This is the sense of this Hebrew phrasing. Daniel Creswell described this type of waiting as "vehement solicitude."[2] This is long-term, tie-a-knot-and-hold-on waiting. Have you been there? Are you standing there now? David empathizes with you, for he knew the feelings and frustrations of prolonged expectations.

We may characterize those who do not wait as "green apple eaters." They couldn't wait until the time was ripe and the fruit was fully ready. Their lives tasted the bitterness of "green apples." Adam and Eve couldn't wait until they tasted the Tree of Life. If they had refrained from the Tree of Knowledge of Good and Evil, they would have existed eternally without knowing the death angel's touch (see Genesis 3:22). Achan couldn't keep his hands off a Canaanite garment and some silver and gold, so he was exterminated. Saul rushed into battle and rushed out of his kingship because he couldn't wait for Samuel's blessing. Judas Iscariot, his messianic expectations shattered by Jesus' servant mentality, couldn't wait for God's conquest to take its rightful course, and so he betrayed his Master and then committed suicide.

One of the classic verses of the Bible is Galatians 4:4: "But when the fullness of time had come, God sent forth his Son, born of woman, born under the law, to redeem those who were under the law" (ESV). God has a timetable, and we must trust Him to do things in the best chronological order for the best results. David waited fourteen years from his anointing to the time he assumed the throne. Joseph waited thirteen years from his sale into slavery until Pharaoh made him the number-two man in Egypt—that's a long wait from the pit to the pinnacle. Jesus Christ, a Man pregnant with power, lived in obscurity until He reached thirty years of age. Then He came forth from some insignificant Galilean town to shake the very foundations of the universe.

WAIT PATIENTLY

"Waiting" is part of God's training process; it is served at His training table. Waiting is a form of spiritual dialysis. We are renovated and revived through waiting.

It is illustrative that the Hebrew word for "waiting" in Psalm 40:1, *qawa*, means "line."[3] I couldn't help thinking of the fishing line. You can't throw your line in the pond and pull it out ten seconds later. David is saying, "I waited and waited for the big one, and finally I caught him!"

As we pursue our agenda during the waiting period, we must be prepared for the chuckles of the opposition. In Psalm 40:15 we find David's foes saying, "Aha, aha." David is steamed about it and prays that God might choke them on their laughter. This double "aha" appears three times in the Psalms, the other two being 35:21 and 70:3. Some scholars relate this to the prophetic passion of Christ.

We must respond in faith to the frivolity of our enemies. I remember when the insurance estimator came to assess the damage to our new church, which had collapsed under the harsh winds and snow of January. As we walked up a wind-bitten hill to the debris, he made this remark: "Reverend, maybe you are praying to the wrong God!" I wanted to push that sarcastic critic to the ground, but I replied something to the effect that God was not finished with us yet. In time, God's work was restored, the people were vindicated and the church had the last laugh!

We are waiting with the knowledge that God is working out His sovereign plan. You see, the dice of life are loaded. Romans 8:28 tells us that desired ends, designed by a divine and loving Father, are destined to become reality. We wait in confidence because we believe and know and stake our victory on a faithful God!

As we are waiting, this psalm reveals that God is working. He is inclining His ear, bringing us out of the miry clay, putting new songs in our hearts and opening our ears to clearly hear His matchless Word.

Is it possible to live with such assurance? This has been personified in many men and women. One such example is discovered in Eugene B. McDaniel, who was shot down over Vietnam. In his book *Before Honor*, he describes his six-year imprisonment in a communist camp. Recognized for his heroism in the face of torture and extreme suffering, he wrote:

> As I grew older in the faith, I came to realize that optimism was solidly rooted in faith in God—the optimism that worked, that is, and any attempt to build up a positive attitude apart from faith could only carry one so many miles. Believing in God's positive attitude toward me, that He wanted the highest good for me, was the only way I could face each day with confidence.[4]

In McDaniel we hear the distant echoes of a man named David: "I waited and I waited and I waited, but I was sure that God was working out His will for my life; I knew that He was thinking about me."

We can say with David, "The Lord be magnified!" With every other substance or living thing, magnification illuminates flaws; with God, it only enhances our awe for His perfection. "Wait, I say, on the LORD" (Psalm 27:14 NKJV).

Compelling Thought

The answer to the question, "How long does it take me to trust God when I encounter a fearful situation?" also answers the question, "How many moments of my life will be spent unproductively?"

Comforting Prayer

Dear Father,
I am a clock watcher. Even though I know that You are never early or late, I often attempt to hurry Your timetable and hasten Your plan. Teach me that waiting is a spiritual discipline, and help me today to exercise that discipline in my daily lifestyle.

Day 16

PSALM 48

Legacy

For this God is our God for ever and ever;
he will be our guide even to the end.

Psalm 48:14

GENE IS A MINUTE PIECE of a chromosome that heavily influences inheritance and development. Genes pass on traits, colors and other characteristics of life forms. There are also spiritual genetics that are transferred from one person to another, passed from one generation to the next. The Jewish people were committed to the older generation mentoring the younger generation, and they made spiritual genetics a high priority in their culture. In his book *Educational Ideals of the Ancient World*, William Barclay cited the three goals for the Jewish father: "to instruct his son in the law, to bring him into wedlock, and to teach him a handy craft."[1] So the Jews told stories and passed on the theology of the one true God through oral tradition (remember, the printing press was not invented until the 1400s).

What are we passing on? Do our little children hear about answers to prayer that redirected our fortunes and reinforced our faith? Are the youth of our time acquainted with the divine moments that emerged because of our heavenly Father's intervention?

In Psalm 48, the sons of Korah, appointed by David to serve as the Levitical choir in the temple, give us a taste of spiritual genetics. In this psalm, they talk about God's royal city (1–3), God's redemptive portfolio (4–11) and God's resilient leadership (12–14). Comparing this to our time and our genetics, we would say that we should talk about the *places* that God has manifested Himself in our lives, the *pictures* where God's redemptive portfolio has been very evident to us as He actively engages in our lives and the *people* who have given us examples of grace-filled, merciful and godly living.

In Psalm 48:1–3, the Hebrews are called to remember God's royal city. It is described as His royal seat, a place of joy, beauty and strength. There is spatial significance for the Hebrews in respect to God's royal city, and in our lives there are those strategic places of divine encounter where we meet with God, where we worship God, where we are convicted by God and then cleansed by God for service to Him. In our lives, we must, like the Jews, call the next generation to the special places of God's indwelling and intervention.

Psalm 48:4–11 features God's redemptive acts. Although the Jewish opponents were unified, the text reminds the reader that these opponents fled in terror. Like the Egyptians, the opponents of the Promised Land were scattered and destroyed. Therefore, by virtue of this record, the Jews hear with their ears and see with their eyes the works of God. In verse 9, they are called to meditate, to picture, to formulate God's scrapbook. In verse 10, it is reported that because of God's acts, His praise extends to the far corners of the globe.

Also, there is reference in Psalm 48:12–14 to God's resilient leadership. We are charged by the Lord in verse 13 to leave a legacy of faith for the next generation and to tell the narratives of His divine work among us. Not to do so is to handicap the next generation, moving them further away from Him and from His actions in their lives. A very interesting Hebrew formation is found in verse 14, and in it we are told this God is forever and ever, and He will be our Guide even to the end. Three different Hebrew words testify to His permanence. This is a great God, the one true God, most worthy of praise. This eternal and everlasting God exists in contrast to the plants around us and the skies above us and the oceans before us, which are all limited and finite and mortal.

Each generation must commit to making sure that the next generation understands the true and right concept of God. If those genetics are passed on correctly, the next generation will have a much greater opportunity to become a generation of righteous people who manifest integrity and holiness before their world. The spiritual genes are being passed on, and so the question must be asked, What kind of genes are they?

Compelling Thought

The answer to the question, "What type of spiritual genes are being passed on to the next generation?" also answers the question, "How much will God's people impact the next generation?"

Comforting Prayer

O Lord,

Help me to pass the baton of blessing to the children and grandchildren of the next generation, to make absolutely sure that they are connected to their Creator and Savior. I do have stories to tell to young minds and soft hearts. May these glimpses of God not remain hidden, but be released to inspire a new inventory of strong and courageous disciples!

PSALM 51

Whiter Than Snow

Wash away all my iniquity
and cleanse me from my sin.
For I know my transgressions,
and my sin is always before me.

Psalm 51:2–3

S DAVID SINGS for us in Psalm 51, it is the autumn of his biological life. He is fifty and counting. His youth is behind him, his twilight years before him. In this psalm it is also autumn in David's soul. The tree that boasted luscious leaves and ornamental fruit is now barren, standing in the midst of brown foliage and rotten crops. David is now singing, "Lord, bring back the springtime."

David's affair with Bathsheba had collected sinful baggage. He had lied, conspired and murdered. It had tarnished his testimony and still mars the majesty of his monarchy. Someone has said, "Sin is like a greased slide. Take one step, and the next thing you know, you are at the bottom looking up." This is the psalm of a king on his knees in the mudhole. Sin has heaped dark clouds of anguish on top of his life. His tears are many, and his pillow at night has become like a stone; sunny days bring no consolation to his inner man.

The first twelve verses of Psalm 51 comprise a classic course in confession. David communicates insights that we can apply to our own times when we ask in faith for forgiveness because we know we have blown it, and blown it badly.

David is tormented and tortured by his sins. His approach to God opens with an immediate appeal to the mercies of God. God's mercies are in multitudes, and that thought counteracts in David's mind the multitudes of sins he has accumulated. He forsakes his own merit; he lays aside his crown; he assumes the kneeling posture of the publican in Luke 18:13, who prayed, "God, be merciful to me a sinner!" (KJ21). Jesus told of this man's justification, and likewise the future held the same destiny for David as he threw his dilemma onto the grace of God.

It is crucial to note that David did come out and acknowledge his sin. In Psalm 51:3 he is explicit in his self-condemnation. Many brothers and sisters have stood on the front porch of forgiveness. They have seen their violations, they are aware of the consequences, but they cannot confess—and this act is the key to the front door through which God takes back the disobedient.

A strategic theological thesis surfaces in Psalm 51:4. David sees sin as an offense to God. A pure, holy, righteous God has been the object of his errant activity. When Joseph was tempted by Potiphar's lustful wife, Joseph refused her overtures by saying, "How then can I do this great wickedness, and sin against God?" (Genesis 39:9 NKJV). The prodigal son's reply to his father as he returned home was phrased like this: "Father, I have sinned against heaven and against you. I am no longer worthy to be called your son" (Luke 15:21).

As we view sin as an affront to the Most High God, who stands as pardoner and executioner, we sense its grim consequences to our lives if it remains unconfessed. We must take our eyes off our existential, horizontal world, and look up to an eternal, ineffable, only wise God.

David's solicitation for purging by hyssop is a direct flashback to the cleansing of a leper. In Leviticus 14:52 a leper's house is sprinkled with water and blood with a hyssop instrument in order to be cleaned.

His reference to being "whiter than snow" is one of the most graphic expressions of forgiveness in the Bible. Snow is so white that it is sometimes difficult to even gaze upon, and the cleansing that David seeks exceeds that of new-fallen snow. Isaiah 1:18 (AMP) is the best-known expression of this analogy:

> "Come now, and let us reason together,"
>   says the LORD.
> "Though your sins are like scarlet,
>   they shall be as white as snow;
> though they are red like crimson,
>   they shall be like wool."

Scarlet is the most difficult color or stain to remove from fabric, yet when the Lord is finished, the fabric's hue is a magnificent white. Hallelujah!

As this psalm unfolds, David seeks an anointing that leads to full acquittal from his pain and spiritual suffering. His ears want to hear the joyful sounds of life again. His bones want to be mended (v. 8). He wants the creative God to construct a clean heart, and to renew a healthy, steadfast spirit within his breast (v. 10). He does not want to be expelled from God's presence, nor have the Holy Spirit sent away from him (v. 11). He passionately longs for the joyful bells of salvation to resound throughout the landscape of his life (v. 12). And history's hindsight confirms that the gracious God responded to David's agonizing confession and lifted him up from disgrace to a new relationship with his loving Lord. David's feet danced again in the celebration of a man whose guilt was vaporized by the love of God!

Compelling Thought

The answer to the question, "Did I confess my sin?" also answers the question, "Is it winter or spring in my heart?"

Comforting Prayer

Dear merciful Father,

I approach Your purity with my impurity, Your holiness with my hollowness, Your perfection with my flagrant imperfection. Please let the snows of grace blanket and cover the darkness of my rebel heart. I long to dance again and praise Your acts of love that transform my despair to delight, and my brokenness to wholeness.

PSALM 51

Restorer

Then I will teach transgressors your ways,
   so that sinners will turn back to you.
Deliver me from the guilt of bloodshed, O God,
   you who are God my Savior,
   and my tongue will sing of your righteousness.

Psalm 51:13–14

IN LESS THAN A YEAR, David has taken a nosedive from the joy of victory to the agony of spiritual defeat. His spiritual stock has plummeted further than a stock market crash. His afternoon gaze upon an incredibly beautiful woman named Bathsheba led him to leave a trail of sin that would shock even the contemporary mind. David fell from the penthouse to the poorhouse.

Psalm 51 distinctly divides into two sections. The first twelve verses major in David's petitions to God to remove the sins that have contaminated his soul. Adultery, lying, drunkenness, murder—can this be the slayer of Goliath, the accomplished musician, the unifier of kingdoms? Yes, it can, and yet David looks to his God for an answer to his anguish. His heart of stone has now turned to water, his pride has been exchanged for humility, and his angry lips now acknowledge his many sins.

The final seven verses of Psalm 51 show the upside of David's unfortunate lapse into sin. He is anticipating a day of deliverance, a recital of praise, a type of worship that is true, authentic, and most of all, acceptable to God. There is a bright tomorrow for sinners who will "cash in their sinful stock" and see their spiritual broker, Jesus Christ. Crashing can be followed by cleansing. It's snowing in heaven, even today, and our confessions unzip God's skies of mercy and grace. Let the snows come and let them cover the soiled landscapes of our hearts. David found out that *grace can erase disgrace!*

As David turns the bend in this confessional psalm, he antici-pates a teaching ministry: "Then I will teach transgressors your ways, so that sinners will turn back to you" (v. 13). David is going to cash in on the school of experience. His fall will lead to others' faith. Paul labeled himself

RESTORER

"the chief of sinners" (1 Timothy 1:15 NKJV), yet he became the greatest teacher of Christianity in the history of the Church.

Think over the words of Jesus as He addresses an overconfident Peter who is about to eat his words of intense allegiance to his Master by denying Him repeatedly. Our Lord turned to Peter and said, "And when you have turned back, strengthen your brothers" (Luke 22:32). Peter's confession and repentance would put him in a place where he could encourage others who had fallen.

David would not waste this lesson on himself, and neither should we miss an opportunity to instruct others through the priceless lessons learned through the grid of our temporary failures. David is going to teach, and beyond that, he is going to testify of God's righteousness. His sins had muzzled his mouth and trapped his tongue. God expects this kind of "out loud" dividend when He forgives. He does not forgive us solely for our own benefit, but so that we may spread His awesome love abroad through the witness of our words. When was the last time you shared from the depth of your heart what God means to you or has done for you? God does not depend on a silent majority! We are to be a vocal majority.

David's anticipatory posture of complete forgiveness not only inspired him to teach and testify, but also to worship in truth. For many months he had worshiped like the Pharisees, who walked around like whitewashed tombs—pretty on the outside, but inside housing dead men's bones.

David shared in verses 16 and 17 the thesis that God does not delight in sacrifices offered by people who are not pure in heart. In other words, the human heart bleeding is better than the animal bleeding.

When David speaks of a broken and contrite heart, he uses a Hebrew word for "contrite" that means "to break; crushed."[1]

David brings a shattered heart to God, which makes his sacrifices legitimate and legal. Spurgeon said: "A heart crushed is a fragrant heart."[2] David knew this well and wrote it into the theology of this confessional: "A broken and a contrite heart, O God, you will not despise" (v. 17 ESV).

You can fool some of the people some of the time, but you can't fool God one single, solitary time! True religion springs from a right relationship with the Father in heaven. And that right relationship is only possible because God's grace can erase our disgrace. "His love has no limit, His grace has no measure,"[3] as the old song says.

I found a prayer by F. B. Meyer to which I believe David would shout "Amen!"

> If my soul has turned perversely to the dark;
> If I have left some brother wounded by the way;
> If I have preferred my aims to thine;
> If I have been impatient and would not wait;
> If I have marred the pattern drawn out of my life;
> If I have cost tears to those I loved;
> If my heart has murmured against thy will, O Lord, forgive.[4]

David's story had a heinous beginning, a hurtful middle as he wrestled in anguish, but a holy ending. He knows his heart has been shattered like a mirror hit by a sledgehammer. He knows that God has promised to forgive this type of confession. Don't chastise yourself for your sins, don't chain yourself with their memory and don't spray yourself daily with their dingy odor. Come and appeal to God's mercies and let the invisible mantle of "heavenly snow" cover your life, so that you will teach, testify and worship Him in Spirit and in truth!

Compelling Thought

The answer to the question, "What happens following God's forgiveness of my sin?" also answers the question, "How many sinners will I teach?"

Comforting Prayer

Dear Restorer of the fallen,

I bow my heart low before You, submitting myself as one who stumbles too often and fumbles too many times in the game of life. In the next few moments, refurbish my tainted soul so that I might testify to others that You have re-created in me a new heart. May I regain the teaching credentials of an obedient disciple and lay aside the sad legacy of a wayward child.

Day 19

PSALM 56

From Fear to Faith

> When I am afraid, I will trust in you.
>
> Psalm 56:3 CSB

FEAR IS A FOUR-LETTER WORD. It is a threat to our worship of God; in fact, if our fears grow large enough, they will dominate our lives and usurp our faith in the one true God. That is why God is so anti-fear.

If one verse were to be lifted out of this psalm as the primary text, it would be verse 3. It is often included in the little Scripture books for children sold in Christian bookstores, as well it should be. It was a part of our Bible memorization program in the early 1960s at the church I attended, and I'm glad it was. It is a good verse for both children and adults to learn, because it addresses a crucial aspect of the Christian life.

This verse acknowledges that Christians do have experiences that breed fear into their breasts, but it also promotes a cure: "When I am afraid, I will trust in you." We are challenged to stop looking at the fearful things and start casting our destiny on a faithful and loving God!

The background of this psalm is found in 1 Samuel 21. David proceeds to the city of Nob and meets with Ahimelech the priest. He is hungry and asks for bread. Unfortunately, the priest does not own a bakery, and the only source of this commodity was the worship bread, also known as the shewbread, which was kept inside the temple. The priest gives David this special bread, because it is being replaced with new hot bread.

David makes a second request of the religious figure. He is in need of a sword, to which Ahimelech replies, "The sword of Goliath the Philistine, whom you killed in the Valley of Elah, is here" (v. 9 AMP). David receives this famous saber and resumes his flight from King Saul.

However, he runs from Saul right into the Philistine army—a classic example of "jumping from the frying pan into the fire." Imagine David trying to disguise himself from the Philistines of Gath, especially since he is now in possession of Goliath of Gath's sword! The servants recognize him. What will he do?

He does not challenge the king of the Philistines, as he did the gladiator Goliath. He does not scream, "The battle is the Lord's!" He resorts to an Oscar-winning performance. As I described for you in Day 13, David acts like a madman before this royal personage, making marks on the doors of the city gates with his fingernails and letting saliva run down his beard. The king labels him insane, and is so disgusted that he lets him escape because he does not want this bizarre personality in his home. It was not pretty, but it worked, and David begins again his trip toward the throne of Israel.

Out of this Halloween-like experience, David pens a psalm detailing his dilemma, which resulted in a frightened hero being delivered in an unorthodox way. David was fearful. He admits to this fact in Psalm 56:3. The word he uses for "fear" is a fascinating one. It is first used in the Bible in Genesis 3:10, when Adam tells God that when he heard God's voice in the Garden after tasting the forbidden fruit, he was afraid.

This word for fear, *yare*, is used not only in negative ways but also to express reverence.[1] It spans the emotion of fear, as well as the mental anticipation of trouble, and also reverence or awe, righteousness or piety, or formal religious worship. Interesting, isn't it, that fear and faith are related? What we fear can become for us a worship experience. Fear and faith are cousins.

David's fears were legitimate. The psalm reveals that his slanderers are pursuing him all day long. They twist his words. They have devoted their lives to creating a successful conspiracy to derail him and destroy him. They are committed to ambushing him and severely altering his destiny. David's fears were rooted in a frightening reality, but it was not a reality that preempted the presence and Person of the Most High God.

In the twenty-first century, our fears are just as real and just as justified. We face such Philistine enemies as prolonged sickness, vocational distress, monetary shortages, unsaved family and friends, sometimes even the assaults of brothers and sisters in the family of God. We must confront these challengers and challenges. If we are going to witness effectively to a world that is lost, and if we are going to impact family, friends and church, we must divert our energies from fearing the secondary sources of our security and invest our faith in a God who is in control.

David's solution is simple to discern. He appeals to the mercy of God in his opening words: "Be merciful to me!" Our Lord loves to demonstrate His mercy. By appealing to His endless, infinite

from fear to faith

storehouse of mercy, we open the door for God to display His beautiful character in an ugly situation.

David transfers his emotions from a fear tract to a faith tract in verse 3. This is the antidote, the answer: The greater our faith, the smaller our fear. And faith dissolves doubt, as the morning sun dissolves the morning fog.

David reaffirms his trust in God, and then makes a crucial affirmation: "I shall not be afraid. What can mere mortals do to me?" (v. 4 NASB). There are people who can wound us, even kill us. Yet David displays almost an arrogance about this. He knows that God can preserve him if He so chooses.

We sometimes fear to the point of weeping, and our prayers rise with salty tears to the heavens. David requests that his tears be put in a bottle (Psalm 56:8); some translations use the word "scroll." The thrust of David's request is that there be a record kept. God knows all your pain; it is as precious to Him as fine wine. Have you ever cried enough to fill a bottle? Remember that a God who cannot forget remembers those tears.

David gets a hold of himself in this psalm and realizes that God is on his side. Psalm 56:9 conveys the assurance of this passionate believer that his prayers will be answered.

The Bible tells us that we live in a physical world, but the ultimate realities are spiritual. We do fight battles, but if we dig deep enough, we will discover that they are all spiritual in nature.

David completes his psalm with thanksgiving and praise. He is looking over his shoulder in Psalm 56:13, seeing another recital of God's saving power. He has emerged out of the darkness of despair to the light of the living.

If the Lord is in your life, you will still experience fear, but that fear will be dismissed as you gaze upon Him and replace your fears with faith in His character! If the Lord is not in your life and you do not know Him personally, then you have a right to be afraid, and your fears should be terrifying, because you will stand alone at the Day of Judgment.

Compelling Thought

The answer to the question, "When I am afraid, whom do I trust?" also answers the question, "How quickly is fear chased from my mind and heart?"

Comforting Prayer

Dear Lord,

There are times when my fear grows slowly and other times when it spikes dramatically. I know these times will come to me and I cannot sidestep their reality. Give me the courage to step from fear to faith! May the darkness give way to the dawn because of my trust in You!

Day 20

PSALM 71

My Rock and My Fortress

Do not cast me away when I am old;
do not forsake me when my strength is gone.

Psalm 71:9

MY WIFE HAS SPENT most of her nursing career in geriatric care, that is, the care of the elderly. Advances in medicine have extended the lifespan of humans, but that translates into coping with old age and all its downsides for an increased number of years. Living into our eighties or nineties does not guarantee a great quality of life or even new bricks added to our noble legacy. I remember that Vance Havner once prayed, "Lord, don't let me live long enough to do something stupid and that's what I'll be remembered for." I think many people can attest not only to the humor of that prayer but to its validity. Psalm 71 is the Senior Psalm, addressing the uncertainties of living in the winter of life.

In the first verse, this senior saint requests that he not be put to shame. In verse 4, he does not want to be squeezed by the hand of the wicked one. In verse 7, he does not want to become a sign to many, a potent, an omen, a black cloud in the sky. And in verse 9, he pleads that he will not end up a castaway, depleted of strength and considered God-forsaken. In these early verses of the psalm, the author clearly communicates the challenges of his senior years.

Who comes to the rescue of this senior citizen as he faces these many challenges? The resounding answer is found throughout the psalm. The Lord is his refuge (v. 3), his rock and fortress (vv. 2–3), his hope since his youth (v. 5), indeed, from the womb (v. 6). This saint boasts of a Lord who is sovereign (v. 16), and who stands as his righteousness (v. 19). It was Calvin who said,

"This does not here denote the free gift by which He reconciles men to Himself, or by which He regenerates them to newness of life; but His faithfulness in keeping His promises."[1] In verse 20, the psalmist portrays the Lord as his restorer. In verse 22, the Lord is the Holy One of Israel. There is a solution to this senior's dilemma, and it resides in the Person of God who is a refuge, a rock, a fortress, a hope, the sovereign, the righteous, the restorer, and the Holy One of Israel.

What is the lifestyle of the senior citizen? We find this senior saint of the psalm praying (vv. 1–4), trusting (v. 6) and praising the Lord (v. 8). We are reminded of Augustine's words, "A Christian should be an alleluia from head to foot!" He is hoping (v. 14), proclaiming (v. 16) and passing it on (v. 18), leaving his legacy to the next generation. The Senior Psalm conveys that it is possible to be a lifetime apprentice in God's Kingdom. The learning never has to conclude, and the service to God never has to end!

In this era following the resurrection of Jesus Christ, the contemporary Christian serves a Savior who is present in all seasons. In an age when so many commitments have a short shelf life, every disciple of Jesus Christ can be encouraged that He will be with us to the end of the age (Matthew 28:20). Our Lord is present with every Christian in the winter of his or her life. Truly He is *Immanuel*, God with us, even when the leaves have fallen off the trees and the snow covers the landscape of our lives.

Compelling Thought

The answer to the question, "What will be the quality of the winter years of my life?" also answers the question, "Will I walk through those December days with Jesus Christ?"

Comforting Prayer

Dear heavenly Father,

When winter comes, I still want to be faithful and bear fruit. I ask humbly that Your Holy Spirit would be strong in me and that Jesus would lead me through the latter days of my earthly journey. Let my despair dissolve in the reality of Your presence and promises.

Day 21

PSALM 73

My Portion Forever

> Whom have I in heaven but you?
> And earth has nothing I desire besides you.
>
> Psalm 73:25

SAPH LED ONE OF KING DAVID'S Levitical choirs. He is the author of Psalm 73, and within its boundaries he wrestles with one of the most troublesome and debilitating questions the believer faces: "Why do the wicked have it so good?" The wicked men of his day had the "wish list" of the righteous. They were prosperous, their bodies were healthy, they appeared free from the common burdens of humankind, people turned to them for advice and counsel and they personified success. These positive realities for the ungodly of his time disoriented Asaph because, although many of his days were spent seeking to pursue God and to follow His commandments, he could not claim as much prosperity and apparent favor as those who disobeyed the Lord!

How do the children of God cope with the contemporary blessings of unbelievers who flaunt their success before them? It is no easy task, as evidenced by Asaph's honest and transparent confession. In verse 13, he goes as far as to say that it is not worth anything to invest in a pure heart or to keep one's hands clean!

However, by the end of his writings he has changed his opinion and reaffirmed that the Lord is the most valuable asset of his life, and the pursuit of God's will is the greatest and most worthy adventure of his life. What changed him?

The attitude of the heart determines the character of the life. Asaph's heart moves back and forth throughout the psalm. He declares that the Lord is good to the pure in heart (v. 1), but he will declare heart purity as vanity (v. 13). Asaph describes his heart as grieved and embittered (v. 21), but he later proclaims that God is the strength of his heart (v. 26). Which is it, Asaph?

If we reflect on our own personal experience, it is both! The heart is moved by the circumstances of life, sometimes to despair, sometimes to delight. At times, the believer wavers; at other times, the believer is as strong as steel in his or her commitment to God. The circumstances of life will endeavor to seduce the believer away from God, but the believer who turns to God, whose heart is set upon the Lord, who makes his or her way to the sanctuary (v. 17), who comes to an understanding of God's nature—that believer will not wither during the adversities of life but will rise above them and move beyond them.

Asaph, though disturbed by pagan prosperity, would shift his focus from the horizontal to the vertical, from the things that other people possessed to the benefits of his God. When he focused on God, he knew that the Lord was always with him (v. 23). The Lord was his guide in this life (v. 24), and even into the glory of the life to come (v. 24). The choir director declared that the Lord

my portion forever

was the strength of his life (v. 26) and the ever-present refuge of his existence (v. 28). Asaph teaches us to look beyond the obvious to the actual!

The saints of every generation struggle with the luxury and leisure of the unbeliever. But Asaph reminds us that we must have the long view of profit and loss. He shows us the ultimate destruction of these who are independent and resistant to God's love. He describes them as on slippery ground (v. 18), and as phantoms and fantasies (v. 20).

It is so imperative to remember that we are grasped by God's right hand (v. 23), guided by His counsel (v. 24) and chauffeured by Him into His glory (v. 24)! At the intersections of our lives, we must hold Him the highest, value Him as the best and trust Him the most! In the end, the believer wins! Don't settle for second best.

Compelling Thought

The answer to the question, "Who or what is first in my life?" also answers the question, "Who or what is second in my life?"

Comforting Prayer

Dear sovereign Lord,
Keep me from judging people's prosperity by what they hold in their hands or what they have in their bank accounts. You can do whatever You want, whenever You want, with whomever You desire. I ask that You sustain me when times are lean and remind me that You are the Source of all that I have when times are good.

Day 22

PSALM 84

A Day in Your Courts

How lovely is your dwelling place,
   LORD Almighty!
My soul yearns, even faints,
   for the courts of the LORD;
my heart and my flesh cry out
   for the living God.

Psalm 84:1–2

ALL OF US HAVE LONGED for something or someone in our lives. This longing was translated into a heated desire, and we found ourselves interrupting others to talk about the object of our desire. This longing crystallized our strategy. This longing, in plain and simple terms, took over our lives.

In August of 2000, over a hundred trapped sailors had a desperate longing for something—oxygen. A Russian nuclear submarine, the *Kursk*, was disabled below the surface in the Barents Sea. Fresh air was normally supplied by power from the ship's nuclear reactor, but when the reactor stopped functioning, the air stopped flowing. Five hundred feet below the surface, one hundred men were not just wishing, not just hoping, but longing with the drive of a drug addict to satisfy their need for air. History confirms their longing was not fulfilled.

In this psalm, the sons of Korah have provided for us the story of a man whom I believe is trapped in a circumstance that prohibits him from satisfying the desperate drive of his heart, namely, to dwell in the presence of God. For whatever reason—and we cannot be certain of the reason—he is not permitted or is unable to make the journey to the temple to worship God. This man longs, yearns, even is about to faint, because he cannot satisfy the hunger and thirst of his soul. He has an appetite not only for God, but also for the place where God is worshiped. This is the addiction of his life, to gather and glorify God with his brothers and sisters of the faith.

Fortunately, there is free access to God, and in our country, free access to the place where saints gather to worship. Access is not the problem, but the attitude of the heart may be. Let's journey through this psalm to harvest the incredible spirit of the writer, and recommit to have this spirit resident in our own hearts, minds and daily agendas.

The description of the Lord as Almighty brings contrast to the forefront, for the writer is in a state of dire need, but if God is Almighty, and He is, this Almighty One can change our bankruptcy into bounty, our catastrophe into a cause for celebration and our death into life, which is quite the metamorphosis.

If you have ever been in love, you have experienced the insatiable thirst for relationship with your lover. If you have ever run out of water on a humid July day, you have experienced a yearning

A DAY IN YOUR COURTS

for ice water. If you have ever been in the hospital for more than a week, you have known firsthand the desire to be home. Our psalmist has known that type of hunger and thirst, and he has an appetite, not only for the Person of God but for the place where God is revered and worshiped.

The psalmist is reminded of the small and tiny sparrows that rest in the eaves of the temple. This memory sparks even more praise of the place where the Lord is worshiped. At the moment he cannot be there, but he pronounces a blessing upon all those who are dwelling there and ever-praising God.

The word for "those" in verse 5 is *adam* (man). Two commendations are given: (1) the searcher's strength is found in his God; (2) the searcher's heart is set on the pilgrimage.

Baca in verse 6 is similar to the verb "to weep." The singular of the word is translated "balsam trees" or "aspens," which are trees that grow in dry, arid places.[1] They dig blessings out of hardship, which is like digging a well in the desert so that others can be refreshed.

God continues to supply the psalmist's needs, and so his strength continues to be replenished by God. The pilgrim resorts to prayers and returns to the theology of an omnipotent, all-powerful, Almighty God.

This longing disciple inserts another incredible statement: "Better is one day in your courts than a thousand elsewhere" (v. 10). He would rather spend one day in the temple than two years and nine months outside the temple.

In verse 11, the focus switches from the king, who is a shield, to the Lord, who is a sun and shield. The word *Almighty* resurfaces in verse 12: "LORD Almighty, blessed is the *adam* [one] who trusts in you."

How can the modern-day saint satisfy this longing in his soul? Here is a five-step application for those who hunger and thirst after God and the place where His people gather to worship Him:

1. Cultivate a lifestyle of worship.
2. Prepare for worship.
3. Talk to others about worship.
4. Pray for God's visitation in worship.
5. Be at worship.

Compelling Thought

The answer to the question, "How hungry and thirsty am I for the presence of God?" also answers the question, "How full of God will my life be?"

Comforting Prayer

Lord Almighty,
I cannot live without You. You are the supreme object of my heart, the primary Person in my life! I rejoice that You have accepted me and drawn me close to Yourself through the Lord Jesus Christ. Lead me often to Your house and sprinkle me—indeed, shower me—with Your glory!

PSALM 90

Teach Me to Number My Days

Teach us to count our days aright,
that we may gain wisdom of heart.

Psalm 90:12 NABRE

T ASBURY THEOLOGICAL SEMINARY, the dean of students made a statement that has stuck like glue to the fabric of my mind. Dr. Robert Traina, speaking to what makes a man successful, answered with a twofold response: "Time and how you use it!"

Time is an exasperating aspect of life. You cannot delay the clock or speed it up. You cannot buy time or give it away. You cannot alter the hours in a day; everyone has twenty-four. It is as if a delivery person arrives at the front door of our life and every midnight hour deposits a package containing twenty-four hours. No one's day is longer than another's. No one's day is shorter than another's. Time is a very inelastic commodity. And yet it is a commodity. It is invested and spent for different purposes and to attain different goals.

In Psalm 90, time is a primary issue. Written by Moses, this is the oldest of all the 150 hymns of the Book of Psalms. It contrasts the eternity of God with the limited tenure of humankind. It begins by revealing three aspects of God in relationship with time. Then it proceeds to depress us with a steady diet of unflattering analogies regarding how much time we really have on this planet. It closes with a needed prayer that challenges each of us to number our days and spend them for God.

It is said that time passes, but actually, we pass, and time stays. I've said, "Time flies," but according to this psalm, a person's life flies, and time is merely the instrument by which he or she measures the flight. In the lifespan that God allows, how will you invest this unpurchasable commodity?

One of the most impressive characteristics of God is the eternal nature of His Person. Food spoils after a time, warranties run out on machines, deciduous trees lose their leaves and evergreens eventually turn to "ever-browns." Books fade in color, carpets lose their pile and records lose their crisp sound. Men and women pass their prime and go through constant metamorphosis; "getting older" does not always mean getting better. In contrast, God was not born, nor will He ever age.

The first two verses of Psalm 90 describe Him as in time, before time and after time. Moses points out to us that God is the dwelling place of His people in every generation. No portion

ME TO ER MY DAYS

of the human caravan found God not at home.

No searcher ever discovered a "no vacancy" sign.

God has always been in attendance, and the divine continuum is a salient fact of human history.

The author informs us that God was before time when he states, "before the mountains were born or you brought forth the whole world" (v. 2). Race back to a time when the elder giants of nature sprung up from the nature's womb, and you will find God. He is the First Cause of all creation. Before there were atoms, there was God. God viewed earth in its infant stages. In glorious contrast is the imagery that God is from everlasting to everlasting. He not only escorts time into being, He bids it farewell. It is God who will tuck time into the scrapbook of history and then nurture His people when they need not track time anymore.

Moses makes a phenomenal statement in verse 4 concerning how God counts time. A thousand years is but a 24-hour period in the eyes of God. On this scale, a 100-year life is equivalent to living 144 minutes. Time is not God's master, but His servant. And we sing so emphatically, "When the trumpet of the Lord shall sound and time shall be no more . . ." Time is mortal in contrast to an eternal, everlasting, endless Deity!

The contrast between God's eternity and humankind's finality is a harsh one to say the least. Verses 3 through 11 cast us into the most lowly and pathetic of analogies. We are destined to destruction. The translation of the Hebrew in verse 3 could be rendered, "Man is turned to dust." We are sent back to the elements, to the habitat of worms. We are ground into the powder of the ground, just as at a burial, the minister will say, "Ashes to ashes, dust to dust."

Humankind is not compared to an oak tree or a blue spruce, but rather to grass. Grass is pretty common fare. It boasts of life in the early morning dew but drags its posture in the afternoon sun. It is easily mowed down, and so life's scythe cuts through our existence like a hot knife through soft butter.

A third analogy is found in verse 9, where life is compared to a tale that is told. The story is so quickly over; the book is so soon closed. It was only yesterday that we were in our teen years; it was only last night that we were married. It was only this morning that we cradled our children . . . and now the nest has emptied.

To make it worse, Moses puts a specific tenure on human life. He lived 120 years, so this is not to say that seventy or even eighty is a maximum, but when you think of your life, and if you have reached these plateaus, you realize you have far more behind you than ahead of you. Life is a weaver's shuttle, a vapor that passes away. Shakespeare put it this way:

> Life's but a walking shadow, a poor player
> That struts and frets his hour upon the stage,
> And then is heard no more; it is a tale
> Told by an idiot, full of sound and fury,
> Signifying nothing.[1]

The apostle Paul put it this way: "If in this life only we have hope in Christ, we are of all men most miserable" (1 Corinthians 15:19 KJV).

Our lives also are subject to sinful passions, which lead to sinful deeds, which lead to the strong and stormy wind of the wrath of God. So the brevity of our lives is compounded by the burden of our sins and the resulting discipline. Verses 7, 9 and 11 will not let us forget the anger and wrath and indignation of this eternal God!

There is a gleam of hope, a ray of light in Moses' prayer that comprises the last eight verses. It gets better. You can spend days of heaven on earth. The finale of Psalm 90 is a gift-wrapped petition to God to assist us in the spending of our days and the investment of the commodity of time in such a manner that God is glorified and we are secure in Him.

"Teach us to number our days." That phrase is not telling us to count how many days we have left, but to carefully evaluate how we live and use the time God does give to each of us! He expects dividends. We will enjoy life if we are accumulating dividends—not the gains of silver and gold, but of incorruptible things.

> Only one life, 'twill soon be past,
> Only what's done for Christ will last.[2]

Compelling Thought

The answer to the question, "Did you invest the days of your life wisely?" also answers the question, "Did you ask the Lord to teach you how to use your days?"

Comforting Prayer

Dear Lord of time and eternity,

The sands of time are sinking in the hourglass of my life, but Your existence is everlasting. You have lived through every generation, and You have witnessed every circumstance and situation. Be my mentor in time management so that my days may reap dividends for You and for the Lord Jesus, Your Son and my Savior and coming King!

PSALM 91

Under His Wings

He will cover you with his feathers,
and under his wings you will find refuge;
his faithfulness will be your shield and rampart.

Psalm 91:4

HARLES SPURGEON PROCLAIMED about Psalm 91, "There is not a more cheering psalm."[1] G. Campbell Morgan called it "one of the greatest possessions of the saints."[2] This is a psalm where there are no depths or depressions. It is a continuous celebration of God's providence and protection. It begins in verse 1 with a riveting thought: "Whoever dwells in the shelter of the Most High will rest in the shadow of the Almighty." This word *dwells* can be translated "abides" or "makes oneself at home."[3] Men and women who spend significant chunks of time in the presence of the Holy One are protected and provided for by their landlord, namely, the Lord God Almighty.

The word *shadow* in verse 1 denotes nearness and proximity, a reminder that God is never remote. Our God is a refuge, a fortress, a bodyguard who can keep us no matter who attacks us. If God wants to keep us safe, no one nor any thing can get near us; if God allows us to be vulnerable, I can keep no one nor any thing away. Our God provides 24-hour security. This is a God who stands sentinel in the day season and in the night season. His alarm systems and security personnel work around the clock and are so devoted to us that they will never leave.

Our God is resilient and tenacious in the care of His children. As we read this psalm of protection, insulation and security, we find that we are under the wings of God (v. 4), which are helping, healing and hiding wings. In verse 7, we find that in the midst of a frenzied battle, God can insulate those whom He chooses. In verse 9, we find that if we make Him our refuge, then we have the promise of verse 10: "no harm will overtake you, no disaster will come near your tent."

This does not suggest that we can deliberately put ourselves in jeopardy. Notice when Satan tempted our Savior in the wilderness, the enemy deployed verses 11–12 to solicit Jesus' participation in putting Himself in harm's way so that God could deliver Him. This is a misuse of this wonderful provision of protection. Indeed, Jesus had the imperial guard of heaven nearby. But we are not to deliberately put ourselves in jeopardy and flirt with fire just to see God take us out of the fiery furnace. Yet we do have heavenly bodyguards, as we are reminded in Psalm 34:7: "The angel of the LORD encamps around those who fear him, and he delivers them."

Two conditions are woven into the tapestry of this lovely hymn near its completion. The first is in verse 14: "'Because he loves me,' says the LORD, 'I will rescue him.'" And in verse 15, we find the second: "He will call on me, and I will answer him." Prayer is a privilege and also contains tremendous power because when

UNDER HIS WINGS

we call upon God, we are given access to His resources and to the ability that He demonstrates to deliver His children. In verse 16, the final, climactic verse, we discover this incredible promise: "With long life I will satisfy him and show him my salvation."

A story that was mistakenly attributed to *National Geographic* but is still circulated as legend provided a penetrating picture, especially in regard to the pictorial phrase *under his wings*:

> After a forest fire in Yellowstone National Park, forest rangers began their trek up a mountain to assess the inferno's damage. One ranger

found a bird literally petrified in ashes, perched statuesquely on the ground at the base of the tree.

Somewhat sickened by the eerie sight, he knocked over the bird with a stick. When he struck it, three tiny chicks scurried from under their dead mother's wings.

The loving mother, keenly aware of impending disaster, had carried her offspring to the base of the tree and had gathered them under her wings, instinctively knowing that the toxic smoke would rise. She could have flown to safety but had refused to abandon her babies.

When the blaze had arrived and the heat had scorched her small body, the mother had remained steadfast. Because she had been willing to die, those under the cover of her wings would live.

"He will cover you with his feathers, and under his wings you will find refuge" (Psalm 91:4). As His children, we are the benefactors of His protecting and nurturing love, which should make a huge difference in how we respond and react to the challenges of our lives. Remember the One who loves you, and then be different because of it.

Compelling Thought

The answer to the question, "Where are you hiding?" also answers the question, "How secure are you?"

Comforting Prayer

Dear Lord,

You are my Refuge and Fortress, my Safe Haven and my Hiding Place. Keep me safe in the sunshine and in the storms of my life. Protect, provide and purify my life. Thank You for being accessible to my cries, calls of distress and need.

Day 25

PSALM 96

Sing

Sing to the Lord a new song;
  sing to the Lord, all the earth.

Psalm 96:1

HIS PSALM COULD BE LABELED, "The Great Missionary Hymn of the Bible." The call sounds far and wide for a *global praise gathering*, embracing every continent, every nation, every people, every language—indeed, every person. The first verse of the psalm immediately shuttles the reader to this worldwide rendition of praise. The concept of "new song" points to recent victories and fresh deliverances that demand more and unique praises.

This serves as a remedial lesson for all believers, for often the praise that used to burst from our lips so naturally and frequently in years past slows from a flood to a trickle. What new song can you sing today because of divine moments that have brought you new opportunities and recent answers to your prayers? According to verse 2 of the psalm, this "planetary praise" is to be perpetual.

The sweeping song of praise continues to be featured in verse 3, which gives the imperative to "declare his glory among the nations." The psalm constitutes a missions manifesto and bids every congregation and every believer to reconsider the Great Commission (see Matthew 28:19–20) and the brightness of the missionary flame that should burn in our hearts. This is no time for missionary recruits to dwindle and missionary offerings to shrink; the heart of God, and by extension the heart of His people, must be intentional toward winning the world!

The psalm takes a different turn beginning in verse 4, when the psalmist deals with the question, "Why should we sing to this Deity?" The answer comes in various forms. This Deity is great and is to be feared above all other gods. In other words, He stands alone; He is in a different league. The diminutive is employed by the psalmist in verse 5 when he states, "For all the gods . . . are idols," which could be translated, "For all the nothings are idols." These idols have been made, but the Lord has made the heavens—quite a contrast.

Each generation must deal with the issue of who or what will be worshiped, revered, adored. Each generation must decide to worship the One True God, or to worship what Herbert Schlossberg designated as "idols for destruction."[1] If we trace the investment of our time, talents and treasure, will it lead us to God or to gods?

What should we ascribe to the Lord? What should be identified with Him? All the nations—no exceptions—are to ascribe to Him glory and strength, because *glory is due Him!* The recipients of this psalm are to comply with five responses:

1. Bring an offering.
2. Come into His courts.
3. Worship the Lord in His holiness.
4. Tremble.
5. Say, "The Lord reigns."

In verses 11 and 12, the invitation is extended to the heavens to rejoice, to the earth to be glad, to the sea to resound. Above humanity, below humanity and with humanity, there is to be the glad and ubiquitous song of praise and thanksgiving. Fields are to be jubilant, and the trees of the forest are to sing. This is a diverse and sundry symphony and chorus that directs its worship and gratitude to the great God.

The final verse of the psalm flashes the yellow caution light: "For he comes . . . to judge the earth." Make no mistake, God will meet His entire schedule and fulfill His Master Plan. And there will be a trial, with its pardons and its punishments. It is a time to sing; it is also a time to send others or to go ourselves to the nations, so that the choir is complete, all sections are full. John Wesley remarked, "The world is my parish."[2] The global glory song will only take place when the hearts of God's children beat with His love and passion for lost people. How can they sing to God if they have never heard of Him? Let the choir recruitment ministry take on a new zeal and purpose!

Compelling Thought

The answer to the question, "Do I care if the whole world sings to the Lord?" also answers the question, "Do I understand the heart of God?"

Comforting Prayer

Dear great and glorious Lord,
   I want to declare Your glory across the street and across the sea. Please give me opportunity to share in the winning and building of men and women in my local fellowship and in global missionary endeavors. May my living and my giving be an accurate reflection of Your love and passion for lost people near and far.

Day 26

PSALM 103

Don't Forget His Benefits

Praise the LORD, my soul,
  and forget not all his benefits.

Psalm 103:2

THIS PIECE OF LITERATURE spells out some of the incredible benefits the Lord provides for those who love Him and who access His magnanimous grace. G. Campbell Morgan labeled it "the perfect psalm of praise."[1] For those who embrace this psalm's diverse and sundry reminders of how much God lavishes upon a fallen race, it becomes a motivational message to draw the believer nearer and tighter to Him in dynamic relationship.

The psalm debuts in verse 1 with the word *praise*, which means, in the original Hebrew, "to kneel, to bless, to salute."[2] The reader is invited to reach deep into the chambers of his or her soul and exalt the Provider of so many undeserved favors. The second verse gives instruction that the recipient of the blessings should not be forgetful of what this benevolent and loving God has done.

Verse 3 begins to detail this lavish litany of benefits that reach and enhance the life of the worshiper who was once a rebel. The double use of the word *all* emphasizes the absoluteness of the benefits in reference to (1) the forgiveness of our sins and (2) the healing of the diseases that attack our mortal frames. There are no indelible stains on our soul; there are no unhealable diseases in the human portfolio.

Verse 4 presents a quick and stark contrast. The imagery of slavery and royalty cause the reader to race from the depths of the pit to the pinnacle of the throne room of royalty. We are redeemed from our self-imposed bondage, and we are crowned with love and compassion.

The benefit package of the Lord touches the physical realm again in verse 5. As our desires are satisfied, that leads to our youth being renewed like the eagle's.

The welcome recital of blessing continues in verse 6 with the featured thought that the Lord is attracted to the "down and out-ers," whereas so many in this world are attracted to the "up and inners." This divine proclivity is flagrant in the life of Jesus as He hears the caustic criticism shelled out by the Pharisees over the way He befriends tax collectors and sinners. Divinity does not divorce itself from the oppressed; divinity attaches itself to the oppressed—hallelujah!

Verse 7 discloses the crucial fact that the God we worship de-sires to reveal Himself, not only to great leaders like Moses, but also to the masses, the common crowd that makes up His family. He does this through natural theology, the world He has created, the prophets, the Law, circumstances, the voice and impulse of the Holy Spirit and the visible picture of the Invisible God, Jesus Christ. The Creator intensely intends for His creatures to know Him!

DON'T FORGET HIS BENEFITS

Verses 8–12 paint the portrait of His incomparable, steadfast love. These verses compose a mini-seminar on the love of God. His anger does not come to a boil quickly, but slowly, for it is mixed with compassion and grace. His love does not manifest itself with persistent anger, but with short-lived disappointment. He does not deal out justice as we truly deserve it; rather, He shortchanges the wages we deserve for our iniquities, the perversities of our lifestyle. How great is His love! Extreme analogies are deployed. "As high as the heavens are above the earth" describes the love He pours out upon those who fear Him. As far as the east is from the west measures how far He removes transgressions from the souls once stained by them—hallelujah!

Is it any surprise that those who pursue an understanding of the personality and provisions of God so often end up singing and worshiping and extolling Him? Go ahead—bless the Lord! Pause right now and start applauding His benefits.

Compelling Thought

The answer to the question, "Why should I invest my time in praising God?" also answers the question, "What are His many benefits?"

Comforting Prayer

My compassionate and gracious Lord,

I want to dig deep in the inner part of my soul and excavate great praise and glory to You for the many benefits You escort into my life. Your love is immeasurable, and Your anger is slow to burn toward me. Please accept my gratitude, though it is meager payment for the blessings of my life!

Day 27

PSALM 118

Give Thanks

Give thanks to the LORD, for he is good;
his love endures forever.

Psalm 118:1

SALM 118 CHOOSES to look back and look forward, to take heart from the past and to look with a strong heart to the future. Martin Luther, the catalyst for the Protestant Reformation, labeled this passage as "my chosen psalm" and described it as "the psalm nearest to my heart."[1] It is a thanksgiving hymn, which begins and ends with the theme of thanks. It is a Messianic hymn, because it foreshadows the advent and ministry of Jesus Christ. And it is a liturgical hymn, which has been employed at the time of Passover and is perfectly suited for one group answering another; it is a textbook psalm for a cantor to lead and direct a congregation.

The first four verses serve as a call to worship. There is public praise: "Let Israel say" (v. 2); there is priestly praise: "Let the house of Aaron say" (v. 3); and there is personal praise: "Let those who fear the LORD say" (v. 4). And the content of the praise is, "His love endures forever." The Hebrew word for love, *hesed*, points to a steadfast, resilient, unfailing love, one that has no built-in obsolescence.[2]

The writer of the psalm quickly conveys that his journey with Jehovah has been no ride in the park. Verse 5 details his anguished cry to the Lord. You could technically translate the phrase "out of my anguish" as "out of the narrow gorge." A colloquial way to translate it would be "between a rock and a hard place." Nevertheless, the author races from anguish to admiration, and his conclusion is liberating: "He answered by setting me free" (NCB).

This believer makes a pertinent set of choices in verses 8 and 9: "It is better to take refuge in the LORD" than to trust in man or princes. And despite being surrounded and ringed by his enemies (vv. 10–12), and despite being pushed to his limits, "about to fall" (v. 13), he found mankind's extremity to be God's opportunity!

His thanksgiving then looks back to the deliverance God gave to Israel in Egypt. Verse 14 is quoted from Exodus 15:2, which is the victory song of the Israelites after the Lord drowned the Egyptians in the Red Sea. But the psalmist not only remembers the troubles and triumphs of the past, he also looks to the future, a future that promises to display the same deliverance that God is glorified for in the writer's scrapbook.

The two words *save us* in verse 25 are a translation of the word *hosanna*. And the psalmist looks to the Lord to act redemptively in his future and "give him success." This traveler expects more victories and more scrapbook memories to be forthcoming. His dreams are bigger than his memories. Are your dreams bigger than your memories? Is the best yet to come?

This "hosanna" looks forward to Palm Sunday, to Jesus' entry into the city of Jerusalem, as He prepares to conquer sin and even the final enemy—death! Yes, one day the stone the builders threw away would become the Cornerstone, the cohesive stone, the foundational stone. Look back over your life and reflect on the "rock and hard place" times. Remember how the Lord brought you through the narrowest of alleys. And then, dream and envision a future where He comes again to bring strength, songs and salvation. Look back; look forward!

Compelling Thought

The answer to the question, "Are my dreams bigger than my memories?" also answers the question, "Who is my refuge and the supreme object of my trust and hope?"

Comforting Prayer

Dear Lord,

You are the God of my past, present and future. You command the consequences and results of all the tenses in my history. Thank You for love that is resilient, that endures forever. Make my life a resonating song of praise that proclaims Your reality and redemption to my family and friends.

Day 28

PSALM 119

Your Word Hidden in My Heart

How can a young person stay on the path of purity?
    By living according to your word.
I seek you with all my heart;
    do not let me stray from your commands.
I have hidden your word in my heart
    that I might not sin against you.

Psalm 119:9–11

HE 119TH PSALM is not a favorable choice for after-dinner devotions. It is the "Granddaddy Psalm," comprising 22 eight-verse sections, equaling almost two dozen of the normal psalms in length. It has been called the "Hebrew Alphabet Psalm" because the 22 sections correspond to the 22 letters in the Hebrew language, and each section starts with a word beginning with a letter of the alphabet—the first section with the first letter, and then the second section with the second letter and so on in consecutive order, until the whole alphabet has been given representation.

The Word of God is elevated in this psalm to heights that are unequaled in any other portion of Scripture. Eight synonyms are used for the Word of God, and they appear in all but one of the 176 verses. If you read and meditate on this psalm, you will sense a new dimension of gratitude for God's revelation to humankind and its potential to impact and drastically alter the course of your history!

In verses 9–16, the writer grapples with the issue of sin and its defilement, and what role the Word of God can play in preventing sin and its affliction. Long ago I inscribed in my Bible this little axiom: "Sin will keep me from this book, or this book will keep me from sin!" As you learn to understand the faith, you realize that this statement cannot hold water without some leakage, but for the most part, its truth can render significant gains in the spiritual formation of our lives.

This second segment of Psalm 119 discloses the powerful and prevailing possibilities if Scripture becomes incorporated into the life and work of the believer. In an age characterized by a frantic pace and misplaced priorities, modern man has, for the most part, shelved daily communion with God. In essence, people are too busy and too independent to get "back to the Bible."

The opening verse of this section poses the question of how a young man can "stay on the path of purity" (v. 9). The Hebrew word for young, *naar*, can be translated "shaken off"[1] and would seem to indicate that time in life when a person becomes more dependent on himself than on his parents. This span of life, from God's vantage point, is precarious. Young men and women can stain their life, alter their course and mortgage their future with just a few falls or one major leap. Purity of heart and cleansing of soul can occur by living according to God's Word. The Bible does not have all the answers to every question, but it does have the most important ones.

There is disdain for this book today, and consequently there are lives being blown apart by sin and its empty promises. The Bible is the "Manufacturer's Manual." This is the compass that points you in the right direction. This is the navigator's chart that does not reveal where all the sandbars are located, but as an old ship captain once said, "I know where the channel is, and that will get me safely home."

Are we sensitive to temptation, the traps of Satan and the ambushes of those who would seek to manipulate our lives and squeeze holiness right out of our souls? Verse 11 tells us that a heart saturated with the Word is less likely to stumble and fall short of God's standard.

At today's airports, much attention is directed at detecting metal objects being carried onto planes. As I recently went through the security check process, I was a witness to the harsh buzzer that indicated that, indeed, there was something to be watched and weighed as to its appropriateness. The ability of these metal detectors to uncover bombs and weapons have spared many a traveler an appointment with death.

I believe that a revival of attention to God's Word would lead to massive reforms in our daily living patterns; the Word is God's "metal detector" applied to make us sensitive to unrighteousness in our lives, which can be more dangerous than any bomb or weapon. God dares you to try it and see.

Psalm 119:13 is a litmus test of our interaction with God's Word. The more we absorb it, the more often we declare it! The world is crowded with people groping in darkness, and as we declare God's

YOUR WORD
hidden in my heart

Word, we diffuse light. Later in this psalm it says, "Your word is a lamp to my feet, and a light for my path" (v. 105 WEB).

In our affluent culture, verse 14 is extremely difficult to put into practice. The worshiper writes that the testimonies of God are equal to the riches that he possesses. In ministering to a church executive's dying wife, I was given a rare jewel from her pale lips. She said, "The things I thought were important don't seem as important anymore, and those things I put off now seem to be the most important!" A deep appreciation for God's Word is not something you schedule for retirement or the dismal days of a terminal illness. Grasp the joy of the Word that daily brings festive faith and often convicting challenge to your doorstep.

Will you consider these affirmations in your own life? It doesn't take a voice from heaven or even a miracle to begin to participate in the serious study of God's Word. And it may prevent a catastrophic freefall in your life that causes irreparable damage.

Compelling Thought

The answer to the question, "Do I use the Word of God as my daily compass for life?" also answers the question, "How often do I get lost on my journey?"

Comforting Prayer

Dear heavenly Father,

I am so grateful that You have provided a compass for my life. Your Word is a lamp to my feet and a bright light to my path. Create in me a greater appetite for Your truth so that I can avoid detours and distractions. Prompt me to persist in the hiding of Your Word in my heart!

Day 29

PSALM 139

Omniscient, Omnipresent, Omnipotent

Where can I go from your Spirit?
Where can I flee from your presence?
If I go up to the heavens, you are there;
If I make my bed in the depths, you are there.

Psalm 139:7–8

AVID, THE WRITER OF PSALM 139, had developed an enormous concept of God. How big is your God? This Scripture passage unhinges a door, and those who step through it view an awesome portrait of an Almighty God.

The three descriptives that are standard fare for studying the Judeo-Christian God are *omniscient*, *omnipresent* and *omnipotent*. What do they mean? The prefix *omni-* is often used in contemporary society and comes from the Latin word *omnis*, which means "all."[1] The three words basically mean that God is all-knowing, all-present and all-powerful.

"God knows everything!" That is the message David communicates in the early verses of this hymn. He is an "open book" to God, from whom nothing can be hidden. The Hebrew word translated "search" in verse 1 is used for investigative purposes, such as "searching for treasure."[2] The Lord knows when David sits down and when he gets up. All his movements are monitored.

Before a thought is even conceived, God knows its height and weight, its color and character. Yes, that means He can read our minds; it even means He knows our mind before it exists. This is the omniscience of God. It can be a blessing, since our motives are often misinterpreted. The flipside of omniscience is that God can X-ray our minds and know when we are hypocrites. This God knows when my thoughts are royal—and when they are rotten.

David acknowledges in verse 3, "You discern my going out and my lying down," and he tacks on immediately, "You are familiar with all my ways."

What about our speech? God is aware of every compliment and criticism we utter. He registers every inspirational sentence and every idle word.

Because of His omniscience, God knows where we have been, He anticipates where we will be and He is touching our lives in the present. God can step into all three tenses.

David acknowledges in verse 6 that this species of knowledge is outside his human capacity. The air gets really thin when we try to reach this level of understanding. A. W. Tozer made a consoling statement on this issue when he wrote in *The Pursuit of God*,

> God will not hold us responsible to understand the mysteries of election, predestination, and the divine sovereignty. The best and

safest way to deal with these truths is to raise our eyes to God and in deepest reverence say, "O Lord, Thou knowest."[3]

In the age-old gospel hymn "I Know Who Holds Tomorrow," Ira Stanhill talks about how we don't know much about tomorrow, but we do know who holds our hand today.[4] Both my short-circuited cognition and God's omniscience are givens in this Christian journey!

The all-knowing God is also the omnipresent God. The author poses a question or two aimed at God's relationship with space. As human beings, we are spatially at one place at any particular time. It is of vital importance to our security and sanity that we realize God is not spatially limited. He permeates all realms, all recesses of space, all existence!

David considers both heaven and hell in this forum of God's access. If people could ascend to heaven, would they separate themselves from their Maker? The answer is an obvious no! David then races to the other end of existence, to the land of the dead, where those in opposition to God make their domain, and he asks if descending there would put him out of God's reach. The answer again is categorically no! The psalmist rides this theological wave even further. What if he could catch a ride on the thin morning clouds of summer, those etched wings in the sky? What if he could sail to the uncharted waters of the Philippine seacoast, and dive to the deepest point of the sea's floor? Would God still accompany him and guide him? Yes, his Lord will never leave him nor forsake him!

Omnipresence is taught throughout God's Word. We must live in the light of this theological tenet. If we sin, there is no benefit in hiding in the bushes, like our ancestors Adam and Eve. If God assigns us a task and we catch a boat to Tarshish like Jonah, we will soon discover that *when we try to run away from God, we run into Him.*

The psalmist sweetens this doctrine in verses 11 and 12 by sharing that even the darkness is like light to God. Whatever constitutes your "night season" of life, whether it is an intensive care unit, the midnight of a fractured or fragile relationship, or the sooty, sunless chimney of some stupid or careless sin, there is hope, for God is near.

David seizes the opportunity to broaden his portrait of God by tracing back this treatise of omnipresence to the days of his tenure in his mother's womb. God is Creator, and His wonderful touch is evident in the dark recesses of a mother's womb. Here, God's eye was on the fetus David; He supervised the shaping of the embryo and knitted together the parts of David's unborn body. God's power, His omnipotence, permeated David's life, even before David uttered his first frantic infant cry.

David also shares that the days of his life were written in God's book before they were lived. The diary of David was already on God's shelf before an event in his life had ever transpired. This recognition of God's life-giving power is a crucial one in our age. We have swallowed abortion and choked on God's Word, which clearly speaks of God's moving in the lives of Jeremiah, John the Baptizer and David *while they still resided in their mothers' wombs.* An all-powerful God is looking out for us. He has brought us into this world, He sustains us during our pilgrimage and He will throw us the life buoy when death's cold waves pull us under! We are fearfully and wonderfully made, because He is omnipotent.

The more birthdays we have, the more we understand our humanity. We are frail children of dust, yet God—the immortal, invisible, only wise God—thinks about us. This is food for praise! Psalm 139:17–18 tells us that God thinks so many thoughts about us that they outnumber the sands on the seashore. Do you realize that if God had a wallet, your picture would be in it?

David returns to the searching nature of God in verses 23 and 24, the theme that began this beautiful hymn. His petition is, "Search me, God, and know my heart; test me and know my anxious thoughts. See if there is any offensive way in me, and lead me in the way everlasting."

My knowledge is fragmented; I need God to do the searching of my soul. I sin in many different places, but His pervasive presence in this world makes Him accessible to my prayers of confession anywhere I may utter them. I need His power, His dynamic force, to lead me out of the miry clay and direct me in the narrow way. God, and God alone, can do that for me!

Use the eyes of faith in your life. Open your eyes and use the wide-angle lens to form your view of God—*omniscient, omnipresent* and *omnipotent*. He knows, He is here and He can do it all. If He didn't, wasn't and couldn't, then He would not be God. I'm grateful He is!

Compelling Thought

The answer to the question, "Can I run away from God?" also answers the question, "Is there anywhere God does not dwell?"

Comforting Prayer

O Lord,

I am so thankful that nothing escapes Your eyes, that You are everywhere and that You can do anything You desire. No height or depth challenges You; no power or force threatens You. I am honored to be watched and cared for by such an awesome God. There are no words adequate to describe You. I worship You, and You alone!

PSALM 150

Praise the Lord!

Praise the LORD. . . .
Let everything that has breath praise the LORD.
Praise the LORD.

Psalm 150:1, 6

T IS FITTING THAT PSALM 150 is the final composition of the Hebrew hymnbook. It has the stamp
of David upon it. The word *praise* occurs one dozen
times. All types of instruments are brought into the
celebration of God and His mighty deeds. It is the icing on the
cake as David commends his God and expresses his adoration.

I would remind you that David had much to praise the Lord
for, such as ascending to the united throne of Israel and Judah,
such as slaying the gigantic gladiator from Gath named Goliath,
such as loyal soldiers and compassionate courtiers who took care
of his health as he aged and withered. He had won many battles,
worn many crowns and wooed many beautiful women.

We must never forget, however, that initially the singer was turned against by the king he faithfully served. This psalmist was chased all over the Holy Land. One wife mocked his dancing after battle, two sons conspired to kill him, one of his sons raped his sister and, of course, his humanity caved in to the beauty of Bathsheba, and the result is one of history's most disappointing soap operas.

Yet David, through it all, never lost his praise for his God.

This patchwork-quilt effect is present in our community of faith. As you study Church history, it is replete with highs and lows, saints and crooks, feasts and famines, healing and holocausts. That is why we must pursue the imperative, "Praise the Lord!"

There will never be a week that does not reflect the mixed bag of triumph and tragedy, light and darkness. The command, "Praise the LORD," lifts all of us above the circumstances that will shape our smiles and start our tears.

The Psalms, especially, encourage us to maintain an attitude of praise, affirming God's glory, remembering His great and awesome deeds and forecasting the marvelous ending He will bring to history.

Each of the last five Psalms begins and ends with "Hallelujah." The Lord is trying to drive this point home: *He is worthy of praise,* and when all is said and done, praise will be our everlasting theme.

The word *hallel,* which is threaded throughout the Psalms, means "to shine, celebrate, or boast."[1] We are to boast of God! Its root meaning is traced to deep, abiding gratitude that points to a superior deed or person. This Person is your heavenly Father.

This God transcends space, stretches further than time and is the Creator, the ultimate Sustainer and Provider of eternal, immeasurable and incalculable Life.

Praise the LORD

When you praise Him in the good times, you acknowledge His goodness. But when you praise Him in the bad times, you testify to your trust in Him. Your belief in God will translate into joy in the dark "dog days" of life. When life gives you a lemon, make lemonade. God is in control. He is God and God alone! My family has several excellent seamstresses in its ranks. When they did tapestries, the back side was full of knots and loose strings; however, when you viewed the front of the work, you were often amazed and complimentary of its beauty. We are people of the long view, and as we trust the Lord to be the Master Weaver, though some events seem to be disappointing, we need to remember we may be looking at the underside!

As we prepare to look over our shoulder at the Psalms, I have a few final reflections. This precious part of Scripture is not like vanilla ice cream; it is more like rainbow sherbet. These writings span human experience, which embraces sunshine and shadows, day seasons and night seasons, Christmas joy and funeral grief. Since the Psalms intersect with all the nuances of our lives, they are applicable and relevant and serve as guideposts for our pathways. My prayerful expectation and hope is that they will assist you in becoming the description of the righteous in Psalm 1:3: "That person is like a tree planted by streams of water, which yields its fruit in season and whose leaf does not wither—*whatever they do prospers.*"

Compelling Thought

The answer to the question, "Do I ever look on the other side of the tapestry?" also answers the question, "Will I miss the work of God?"

Comforting Prayer

Dear Lord,

I praise You for Your character and creation! I praise You for all that I know and for all that I can imagine! You are the best of the best, the most excellent, the magnificent God! May my breath be framed in thanksgiving to You, in every day season and night season. I love You deeply, and my heart's desire is to adore You forever and ever. Amen.

NOTES

Introduction

1. John Calvin, from the preface to his *Commentary on the Psalms* (1557).

Day 2

1. Augustine of Hippo, *Confessions* (Lib. 1.1.1).

Day 3

1. Augustine of Hippo, *Soliloquia*, book 2, chapter 1.
2. Charles Spurgeon, *A Treasury of David, Volume I: Psalms 1–57* (McLean, Va.: MacDonald Publishing, n.d.), 95.

Day 4

1. *Eerdmans' Handbook to the History of Christianity* (Grand Rapids, Mich.: Eerdmans, 1977), 608.
2. Herman Dooyeweerd, as quoted by Herbert Schlossburg in *Idols of Destruction* (Nashville: Thomas Nelson, 1983), 14–15.
3. Henry David Thoreau, "Civil Disobedience" (1849).

Day 5

1. John Bates, *Cyclopaedia of Moral and Religious Truths* (1865).

Day 8

1. Vance Havner, *Pepper N' Salt* (Old Tappan, N.J.: Fleming H. Revell Co., 1966; Grand Rapids, Mich.: Baker Book House, n.d.), 9.

2. Augustine, *Confessions* (Lib. 1.1.1).

3. Blaise Pascal, *Pensees* (New York: Penguin Books, 1966), 75.

4. F. B. Meyer, *The Shepherd Psalm* (Chicago: Moody, 1976), 48–49.

Day 9

1. Meyer, *Shepherd Psalm*, 109–110.

2. John Phillips, *Exploring the Psalms: Volume I: Psalms 1–41* (Neptune, N.J.: Loizeaux Brothers, 1985), 175.

Day 10

1. *Lincoln Observed: The Civil War Dispatches of Noah Brooks*, ed. Michael Burlingame (Baltimore, Md.: Johns Hopkins University Press, 1998), 210.

Day 11

1. Spurgeon, *Treasury of David*, 49.

2. Spurgeon, *Treasury of David*, 51.

3. Phillips, *Exploring the Psalms*, 227.

4. Spurgeon, *Treasury of David*, 49.

Day 12

1. Augustine of Hippo, as quoted by John Ker, *The Psalms in History and Biography* (Edinburgh: A. Elliot, 1886), 58.

Day 13

1. Hannah Whitall Smith, *Living in the Sunshine* (New York: Fleming H. Revell, 1906), 203.

Day 14

1. James Strong, *Strong's Exhaustive Concordance of the Bible* (Nashville: Crusade Bible Publishers, Inc., 1890), 1,556.

Day 15

1. Phillips, *Exploring the Psalms*, 305.

2. Spurgeon, *Treasury of David*, 243.

3. Strong, *Exhaustive Concordance*, 102.

4. Eugene B. McDaniel, *Before Honor: One Man's Spiritual Journey into the Darkness of a Communist Prison*, with James L. Johnson (Philadelphia: A. J. Holman, 1975), 61–62.

Day 16

1. William Barclay, *Educational Ideals of the Ancient World* (Grand Rapids, Mich.: Baker, 1959, 1974), 16.

Day 18

1. Strong, *Exhaustive Concordance*, 30.

2. Spurgeon, *Treasury of David*, 407.

3. Annie Johnson Flint, "He Giveth More Grace" (Kansas City, Mo.: Lillenas, 1941).

4. Continuum, *The Complete Book of Christian Prayer* (New York: Bloomsbury, 2000), 259.

Day 19

1. R. Laird Harris, Gleason L. Archer Jr., Bruce K. Waltke, eds., *Theological Wordbook of the Old Testament*, vol. 1 (Chicago: Moody Press, 1980), 401.

Day 20

1. John Calvin, *Commentary on the Psalms*, vol. 3., verse 19.

Day 22

1. Frank E. Gaebelein, ed., *The Expositor's Bible Commentary*, vol. 5 (Grand Rapids, Mich.: Zondervan, 1991), 544.

Day 23

1. William Shakespeare, *Macbeth* V, v, 17.

2. C. T. Studd, "Only One Life, 'Twill Soon Be Past," n.d., https://reasonsforhope jesus.com/only-one-life-twill-soon-be-past-by-c-t-studd-1860-1931.

Day 24

1. Spurgeon, *Treasury of David*, 88.

2. G. Campbell Morgan, *Exposition of the Whole Bible: Chapter by Chapter in One Volume* (1959; repr., Eugene, Ore.: Wipf & Stock, 2010), 255.

3. Strong, *Exhaustive Concordance*, 52.

Day 25

1. Herbert Schlossberg, *Idols for Destruction* (Nashville: Thomas Nelson, 1983), 6.

2. John Wesley, *Journal*, June 11, 1739.

Day 26

1. Morgan, *Exposition of the Whole Bible*, 259.

2. Strong, *Exhaustive Concordance*, 102.

Day 27

1. Martin Luther, from the dedication of his translation of Psalm 118.

2. Harris, Archer, Waltke, *Theological Wordbook of the Old Testament*, 305.

Day 28

1. Harris, Archer, Waltke, *Theological Wordbook of the Old Testament*, 585.

Day 29

1. *Merriam-Webster*, s.v. "omni-," accessed February 8, 2022, https://www.merriam-webster.com/dictionary/omni-.

2. Phillips, *Exploring the Psalms*, 592.

3. A. W. Tozer, *The Pursuit of God* (Camp Hill, Penn.: Christian Publications, 1982), 104.

4. Ira Stanhill, "I Know Who Holds Tomorrow," Singspiration Music, 1950.

Day 30

1. Strong, *Exhaustive Concordance*, 33.

Arnold R. Fleagle has published poetry, written articles for church magazines, and co-authored or authored twelve books, including *The Commands of Messiah.* In his teen years he won several writing awards, including a district youth writing contest (where he was the only entry), first place in a newspaper contest and second place at the Pennsylvania Rotary Leader's Camp. Also, his sermon "The Three Visons of Isaiah" tied for first place in his denomination's message competition.

Arnie has a bachelor of science in education from Shippensburg University, a master of arts in biblical literature from Asbury Theological Seminary and a doctor of ministry from Gordon-Conwell Theological Seminary. He has served as a senior pastor in five churches and as director of development in the Central District of the Christian and Missionary Alliance. He now serves as an interim pastor for that same district.

He has been married to one lady, Faye, and they have two sons, Matthew and Marc. They have the privilege of being Mimi and Pappy to four exceptional grandchildren.

Arnie follows sports at all levels and is a Penn State and Pittsburgh Steelers fan. He collects a number of items, including Christmas nutcrackers, banks, clocks, and milk bottles. His favorite vacation spot is Myrtle Beach, South Carolina.

He became a follower of Jesus Christ at age twelve on April 1, and he affirms, like Paul, "I became a fool for Christ's sake." His purpose in writing is to give clarity to the meaning and power of God's Word and to encourage individuals to accept Jesus Christ as Lord and Savior, and for those already saved, to motivate them to follow Him with courage and obedience.